European
Employment Law

European Employment Law

A Brief Guide to the Essential Elements

Claire-Michelle Smyth

BEP BUSINESS EXPERT PRESS

European Employment Law: A Brief Guide to the Essential Elements

First published in 2017 by
Business Expert Press, LLC
222 East 46th Street, New York, NY 10017
www.businessexpertpress.com

ISBN-13: 978-1-63157-916-5 (paperback)
ISBN-13: 978-1-63157-917-2 (e-book)

Business Expert Press Business Law Collection

Collection ISSN: 2333-6722 (print)
Collection ISSN: 2333-6730 (electronic)

Cover and interior design by Exeter Premedia Services Private Ltd., Chennai, India

First edition: 2017

10 9 8 7 6 5 4 3 2 1

Printed in the United States of America.

Abstract

Within Europe, employment law has grown as a result of regional rather than national legislation. The European Union has been at the fore of developing a comprehensive framework to protect workers from unfair practices and discrimination. In addition to the European Union, the Council of Europe also plays a role in protecting workers. The European Social Charter and the European Convention on Human Rights contain provisions relevant to the employment relationship.

This publication will give the U.S. business student an overview of the key laws governing the area of employment in Europe. Here we look at the obligations and regulations surrounding the contract of employment, the laws surrounding equality and nondiscrimination, and the protection for unions and collective bargaining. Comparisons are drawn with American law and regulation at regular intervals to illustrate different practices within Europe and the United States.

This book will provide the student with knowledge of the essential elements of European Employment Law in a concise and easy-to-understand manner.

Keywords

employment, European Union, equality, nondiscrimination, workers' rights

Contents

CHAPTER 1

Introduction

In today's business market, multinational transglobal entities are increasingly common. In such a global market businesses are not restricted to trading within their own country. Cross border international trade can account for a substantial portion of the business. As its international trade grows, it is likely that the business will have at least one office or hub outside of its country of origin.

In recent decades, Europe has been an attractive place for American businesses to thrive. With many European countries boasting a highly educated population, proficiency in the English language, and low taxes to encourage foreign direct investment, it has drawn many U.S. companies. Top American companies such as Google, Boston Scientific, Intel, Apple, and Facebook have bases in Ireland, and Microsoft, Cisco Systems, and American Express have offices in the UK. As American businesses open branches (and occasionally their headquarters) within Europe, this operation will be subject to European employment law. This law will operate and govern the employment relationship, from the hiring process through the employment contract and conditions of work to dismissal from employment. While there are certain similarities between European and American employment laws, it is of vital importance that the American employer or manager or indeed employee be aware of the employment laws that oversee and manage the employment relationship in Europe.

This guide is aimed at the American business student who may operate in some capacity within the European market and as such provides an overview of the key areas of European employment law. It is not a comprehensive or exhaustive text nor does it incorporate all of the laws governing employment law in Europe. It aims to give an overview of the key concepts, and the interested student is advised to further read the material referenced in the footnotes and bibliography for more in-depth analysis.

First, it is important to understand the sources of employment law within Europe. While they can derive from national law, regionally there are three sources of European Law that seek to harmonize law and practice within the region. While the European Union (EU) is the most assiduous in implementing and imposing employment laws and regulations, the European Social Charter (ESC) and the European Convention on Human Rights (ECHR) also play a role. The origin and scope of each of these three sources is discussed in Chapter 2. Chapter 3 examines the employment contract and sets out what each employee is entitled to in terms of that contract. Unlike America, the EU states that each employee must receive written terms of his or her employment. We consider how the employment contract is formed and what terms must be included in writing. Chapter 4, the lengthiest chapter in this publication, examines equality and nondiscrimination. This is a founding principle of EU employment law and determines that an employer will be in breach where a worker is discriminated against in hiring, working conditions, promotion, and pay on the grounds of sex, race, religion, sexual orientation, or age. The special protection given to pregnant women against discrimination is considered in Chapter 5. Another key aspect of EU law is the free movement of workers. In order to facilitate a free market and enhance productivity it was essential that member states be able to access skilled workers from their neighboring states within the EU. This was the beginning of free movement, which essentially removed any visa or permit requirements to travel and work in another member state. Chapter 6 looks at the evolution of this principle, including access to social welfare for migrating workers. The final chapter provides an example of where the EU does not provide a legislative framework and we look outside of the ESC and the ECHR for trade union rights and the right to bargain collectively.

Comparisons are drawn with American law where relevant and for illustration purposes. Overall, this guide should give the reader an insight into the key aspects of European employment law, including the employer's responsibilities and the employee's rights.

CHAPTER 2

Sources of European Employment Law

In Europe, there are three main sources of employment law: the European Union (EU), the European Social Charter (ESC), and the European Convention on Human Rights (ECHR). This chapter gives a brief overview of the creation, purpose, and scope of each of these sources.

The European Union

Following World War II in an attempt to rebuild Europe, foreign ministers decided in June 1955 to create a common economic institution and, in 1957, the European Economic Community was born.[1] Its sole purpose was to create and harmonize an internal economic market. The treaty created the three institutions of the EU: the Commission (which is the main legislator and has the power to bring states to the Court of Justice of the European Union for noncompliance); the Council of Ministers (who discuss, amend, and adopts laws); and the Parliament (the only directly elected body of the EU, which now has a colegislative role with the Commission). During its first decade, it also created the Court of Justice of the European Union (CJEU) (or the European Court of Justice, as it was then called).

The EU has evolved and its powers increased significantly since its creation, although its core purpose has remained. The EU is an inherently economic institution focused almost entirely on ensuring its economic stability. Business, and consequentially employment, plays an overwhelmingly large role in this and therefore it is logical that the EU would create

---

[1] European Union 1957. *Treaty establishing the European Community (Consolidated Version), Rome Treaty*, 25 March.

laws to regulate both. Initially these legislative measures were concerned with removing barriers to trade and ensuring fair competition, but as their competences grew they became more involved in social cohesion and in developing a social policy. The Treaty on the Functioning of the European Union affirms its objective is to attain full employment while at the same time ensuring just conditions of work.[2]

There are a number of different sources of law within the EU itself and these are hierarchical. Primary sources of law are the treaties of the EU. These treaties create the legal order and they are binding on all member states. They are the superior law of the union and cannot be amended or revised outside the strict procedure set down in the treaties themselves. General principles of EU law are the unwritten rules of law that the CJEU would apply in order to avoid injustice, to fill a gap in EU law, or to strengthen the coherence of the law. As a general rule, they either form part of primary law or sit just below it, but remain above all other sources of EU law. In doing so, the court often draws on principles from established general principles or *jus cogens* of international law, such as the principle of legal certainty and procedural rights. Further, it can find general principles from the national systems of the member states. This does not require all member states to adopt a particular principle; it is sufficient that it is common to several.[3]

Secondary sources of EU law are ranked lower than the treaties and can be in the form of a Regulation, a Directive, or a Decision. Regulations are the most important of the secondary sources as they apply *erga omnes* (to everyone) simultaneously. A regulation has general application, explained in *Koninklijke* as applying "to objectively determine situations and produce legal effects with regard to persons described in a generalized and abstract manner."[4] A regulation is binding in its entirety, and incomplete or selective implementation is prohibited under EU law. Further,

---

[2] European Union 2007. *Consolidated Version of the Treaty on European Union and the Treaty on the Functioning of the European Union*, 13 December 2007, 2008/C 115/01.

[3] Kaczorowska, A. 2013. *European Union Law*, 117. 3rd ed. New York: Routledge.

[4] Case 143/77 *Koninklijke Schilten Honing v Council and Commission* [1977] ECR 797 [21].

a regulation is directly applicable to all member states at the time of its entry into force.

Directives are used to harmonize the law throughout the union. They have no general application unless they are addressed to all member states. They impose an obligation on the state to fulfill a certain objective, but the method of achieving such is left to the member state to decide, as long as it chooses a path that ensures legal certainty and transparency. Directives will give the member state a certain amount of time in which to introduce the necessary law and/or procedure to give effect to the objective. The member state has responsibility to ensure that the directive is incorporated into national law. If the state fails or refuses to implement the directive within that time period, it becomes directly applicable in that member state; an individual may rely on it in national courts and the Commission may bring an action against that state for a breach of EU law.

Decisions, like directives, have no general application unless they are addressed to all member states. Decisions are binding from the date that they are made and against the member state to which they are addressed.

The CJEU as a source of EU law is complex. Its primary role is to interpret the laws of the EU and not create law. However, in practice, it has created law by bringing in general principles of EU law. A salient example of this is how the court has, over time, brought human rights within its scope. Here we can see three distinct phases of the court's reasoning. The first phase is evident in the *Stork* case, where it refused to examine whether EU law was in compliance with the fundamental rights established in national constitutions.[5] One reason for this outcome was based on the concept of supremacy (discussed in the following), but another was based on the fact that the treaties did not contain any reference to fundamental human rights. The court therefore focused on the economic goals, leaving human rights eminently rejected.[6]

---

[5] Case 1/58 *Friedrich Stork & Cie v. High Authority* [1959] ECR 17.

[6] Zuleeg, M.M. 1971. "Fundamental Rights and the Law of the European Communities." *Common Market Law Review* 8, no. 4, pp. 446–61.

The second phase is where the court, following pressure from member states, began to modify its position. In *Stauder*, the court remarked obiter that fundamental rights formed part of the general principles of EU law.[7] This ruling was expanded upon in *Internationale Handelsgellschaft*, which is the first case that formally recognized fundamental rights as forming part of community law as deriving from the national constitutions of member states.[8] In *Nold*, the court enunciated an additional basis for incorporating fundamental rights into community law (supplementary to national constitutions) and into international human rights treaties, in particular the ECHR.[9] However, the court in *Grant* explained that there is a limitation in engaging with human rights, in that those fundamental rights cannot have the effect of extending a treaty provision beyond the competence of the EU.[10]

The third and final phase is the determination that the protection of fundamental rights extends not only to EU institutions but also to member states. This was initially a highly controversial move, given the lack of uniform application of fundamental rights within the member states, but also because of the haphazard development of the case law. This has since been ameliorated with the entry into force of the Charter of Fundamental Rights of the European Union, which gives the court broad powers to scrutinize whether member states are acting in a manner compatible with the human rights.[11]

Under EU law, there is no doctrine of precedent. Previous case law is not binding and the CJEU follows a civil law approach to precedent. The doctrine of precedent, also known as *stare decisis*, is a cornerstone of the common law system and means "let the decision stand." In operation it has the effect of ensuring that lower courts are bound by the decision of

---

[7] Case 26/69 *Erich Stauder v. City of Ulm-Sozialamt* [1969] ECR 419.

[8] Case 11/70 *Internationale Handelsgesellschaft* [1970] ECR 1125.

[9] Case 4/73 *Nold, Kohlen-und BaustoffgroBhandlung v. Commission* [1974] ECR 491.

[10] Case C-249/96 *Lisa Jacqueline Grant v. South-West Trains Ltd* [1998] ECR I-621.

[11] European Union 2012. *Charter of Fundamental Rights of the European Union*, 26 October, 2012/C 326/02.

higher courts, and courts of the same jurisdiction should not depart from their previous ruling unless there is good reason to do so. This ensures consistency and stability in determinations. As the CJEU does not operate on a system of precedent it is very difficult to see how the judgments of the court could form part of the law of the EU, if they are liable to be repealed or changed with every new case. However, in practice, the court does respect its own previous decisions as to depart radically from them would be to undermine itself. Over the years it has played an important role in building up a body of consistent and coherent case laws, setting the benchmark for member states.

Two fundamental principles of EU law created by the CJEU ensure compliance and uniform application of law and principles throughout member states: the supremacy of EU law and also its direct applicability.

The concept of supremacy does not come from a treaty provision. Rather, the court explained the principle and its necessity in *Costa v. ENEL*: "The law stemming from the treaty, as an independent source of law, could not, because of its special and original nature, be overridden by domestic legal provisions, however framed, without being deprived of its character as community law and without the legal basis of the Community itself being called into question."[12]

The position of the CJEU has not changed since this ruling. A fundamental and key concept of EU law is that it is supreme to national law and that such supremacy is necessary in order for the free market to function. This supremacy is effective over national constitutions and international agreements concluded after the creation of the EU.[13]

Thus, the law of the EU is supreme over national law and, where there is a conflict between the two, the member state is legally bound to give effect to EU law and disregard the national law. This is complimented by the second key principle of EU law—that it is directly effective in the national systems of member states. This is another creation of the court considered necessary in order to ensure not only the effectiveness of EU law, but also that individuals deriving benefit therefrom would be protected. Arguably, this concept was first established by the Permanent

---

12 [1964] ECR 585, 594.
13 Case 11/70 *Internationale Handelsgesellschaft* [1970] ECR 1125.

Court of International Justice in *Concerning the Competences of the Courts of Danzig*.[14] Here, it was held that, where a treaty is adopted that creates rights and obligations capable of being relied upon in domestic courts, it provides an exception to the general rule that individuals are not subjects of international law. This principle was adopted by the CJEU in the *Van Gend & Loos* case, where it justified the approach by stating that the Community "constitutes a new legal order of international law... the subjects of which comprise not only of member states, but also their nationals."[15] In order for a piece of EU law to be directly effective, it must meet certain criteria, which have evolved from the CJEU over time. First, it must be clear and precise. Second, it must be unconditional, meaning that it does not require any implementing measures on the part of the member state. Finally, and where relevant, the deadline for implementation by a member state, where such is required, must have passed. This is restricted primarily to directives that depend upon measures being taken by the member state. This principle applies both horizontally and vertically, meaning that the provisions of EU law can be relied upon in national courts against the member state and also against private entities, such as businesses.[16]

In terms of employment laws this means that where the employer has failed to implement an EU law or is acting in breach of EU law the employee can rely on it in the domestic court. Therefore, it is extremely important that the employer be familiar with their obligations under EU employment law.

The European Court of Human Rights

The ECHR, proposed by the Council of Europe,[17] adopted in 1950, and entered into force in 1953, was also created in the wake of World War

---

[14] Advisory Opinion on 3 February 1928, Series B, No. 15

[15] Case 26/62 *NV Algemene Transport- en Expedite Onderneming van Gend & Loos v. Netherlands Inland Revenue Administration* [1963] ECR 1, 12.

[16] The horizontal application was confirmed in Case 43/75 *Defrenne v. Sabene* [1976] ECR 455.

[17] Established in 1949 under the Statute of the Council of Europe ETS No. 001, a top priority for the newly created institution was to develop a Charter of Human

II. While the EU was created primarily with the aim of ensuring peace in the region through economic stability and the rebuilding of national economies, the Council of Europe was tasked with protecting human rights in the region. Internationally, at this time the United Nations had just adopted the Universal Declaration on Human Rights in 1948 and negotiations were on the horizon to transpose this into a legally binding treaty. The ECHR was again a regional response to the war and sought to ensure accountability for human rights violations within its state parties. The ECHR[18] was established, which was empowered to hear both individual[19] and interstate complaints.[20]

The Council of Europe is an entirely separate entity to the EU and the two should not be confused. While the EU was established as an inherently political institution with a primary objective of economic stability, the Council of Europe was primarily concerned with the promotion and protection of human rights. The ECHR contains a number of articles that are relevant to employment law. Article 8, which provides for the right to respect for private and family life, has been interpreted to include matters of occupational health and injury at work. Article 9, which provides for the freedom of thought, conscience, and religion, ensures that no one may be discriminated against on the grounds of religious belief or conscientious objection. Article 11 allowing for the freedom of assembly and association allows for employees to join trade unions and to peacefully protest. Article 14 contains a general prohibition on discrimination that may be applicable in employment matters.

Rights and a court to enforce the rights contained therein. See E. Bates. 2010. *The Evolution of the European Convention on Human Rights: From its Inception to the Creation of a Permanent Court of Human Rights* (London: Oxford University Press) and Mowbray, A. 2012. *Cases, Materials and Commentary on the European Convention of Human Rights*. 3rd ed. London: Oxford University Press.

[18] Initially, the Convention established two part-time institutions; the European Commission of Human Rights acted as a court of first instance that would, in certain circumstances, refer cases to the European Court. Protocol 11 (CETS No 155) replaced these with a permanent court.

[19] Article 34.

[20] Article 33.

Unlike the EU, rights under the ECHR can only be enforced against the state and not an individual. Thus, it imposes an obligation on the state to ensure that employers do not breach their convention rights. Under the admissibility rules of the ECHR the employee would have to first exhaust domestic remedies, in other words they would have to show that they have gone through the national court system first. Where the employee gets no satisfaction from the national courts, they can then apply to be heard in the ECHR.

The European Social Charter

The ESC, which entered into force in 1965, protects only social and economic rights. It is a creation of the Council of Europe and was designed as a counterpart to the ECHR, which textually protects civil and political rights only. Several revisions to the Charter have occurred, culminating in the Revised Social Charter of 1996, which came into force in July 1998.[21] Part I of the Charter lists the rights in the form of objectives, while Part II establishes the corresponding obligations the state must fulfill in order to meet these objectives. Article 20 of the ESC establishes that the state must accept a minimum of 6 of the 9 core obligations. These are the right to work,[22] the right to organize,[23] the right to collectively bargain,[24] the right of children and young persons to protection,[25] the right to social security,[26] the right to social and medical assistance,[27] the right of the

---

[21] Additional Optional Protocols were annexed to the Charter in 1988, 1991, and 1995.

[22] Article 1 "Everyone shall have the opportunity to earn his living in an occupation freely entered into."

[23] Article 5 "All workers and employers have the right to freedom of association in national or international organisations for the protection of their economic and social interests."

[24] Article 6 "All workers and employers have the right to bargain collectively."

[25] Article 7 "Children and young persons have the right to special protection against the physical and moral hazards to which they are exposed."

[26] Article 12 "All workers and their dependants have the right to social security."

[27] Article 13 "Anyone without adequate resources has the right to social and medical assistance."

family to social, legal, and economic protection,[28] the right of migrant workers and their families to protection and assistance,[29] and the right to equal opportunity and equal treatment in matters of employment without discrimination on the grounds of sex.[30] All other provisions are not deemed to be core. The European Committee on Social Rights (previously called the Committee of Independent Experts) oversees the enforcement of the ESC. The Committee does not see the ESC as a mere statement of rights. Rather, its aim is to "protect rights not merely theoretically, but also in fact."[31]

In order to fulfill this supervisory role, states have an obligation to report on the implementation of the ESC rights that they have agreed to be bound by, every two years in respect of core rights and every four years for all other provisions. The Committee then issues compliance reports based upon its investigations of these submissions.[32] It has been argued that this supervision is unsatisfactory in that it, like the reporting system for United Nations human rights treaties, relies solely on the subjective view of the state and arguably an independent assessment would be better.[33] These compliance reports are not legally binding and the Committee has no power to force the state to comply with its recommendations.

The collective complaints procedure was introduced as part of the revitalization of the Charter, which began in 1990. The complaints are also heard by the Committee and therefore the enforcement mechanism for breaches of the ESC is not judicial like the European Court and sanctions

---

[28] Article 16 "The family as a fundamental unit of society has the right to appropriate social, legal, and economic protection to ensure its full development."

[29] Article 19 "Migrant workers who are nationals of a Party and their family have the right to protection and assistance in the territory of another Party."

[30] Article 20 "All workers have the right to equal opportunities and equal treatment in matters of employment and occupation without discrimination on the grounds of sex."

[31] *International Commission of Jurists v. Portugal,* Complaint No 1/1998, Decision on the merits, 9 September 1999.

[32] Harris, D., and J. Darcy. 2001. *The European Social Charter,* 310. 2nd ed. New York: Transnational Publishers.

[33] Martin, N. 2009. "Forty Years of the European Charter: Celebration or Commiseration." *University College Dublin Law Review* 1: 67.

cannot be imposed on states. The recommendations and decisions are not enforceable and, thus, a violation may continue for years before any changes are made by the state to make it compliant with its obligations. Enforcement of Charter Rights relies mainly on political pressure, naming and shaming states that are in breach by publishing their reports to ensure that obligations are fulfilled.

The ESC identifies four groups that are permitted to bring a complaint before the Committee: (1) international organizations of employers and trade unions; (2) NGOs that have consultative status with the Council of Europe; (3) national organizations of employers or trade unions within the jurisdiction of the state against which they have lodged a complaint; and (4) (for states that have accepted the provision to allow NGO's to take a complaint) other NGOs with particular competence in the matter complained of.[34]

From the list of groups entitled to bring a case to the Committee it is clear that the focus is very much on employment and related matters.

As we can see earlier, there are three separate systems from which European employment law derives. As we go through the various chapters you will see that EU law plays the lead role, however the other two are certainly not to be dismissed. They confer rights on employees and citizens that the state must protect. The state does this by putting measures in place to ensure that employers respect these rights afforded to employees. Where the employer fails to do this, the state must step in and remedy the breach. If the state fails to do this it could find itself before the ECHR or the European Economic and Social Committee (EESC), or indeed the CJEU. As we have seen, EU law is different from the ECHR and the ESC as it applies both horizontally and vertically. In other words, you can take your employer to court for breach of rights derived from EU law. It will become evident in the coming chapters that EU law gives particular employment rights to individuals. While the individual is conferred with these rights it is the state that must implement them. Therefore, where the state fails to implement or enforce EU law, it is responsible to the individual. This is logical; if the state is not held accountable for its breaches

---

[34] Additional Protocol to the European Social Charter Providing for a System of Collective Complaints, Strasbourg, 9 XI 1996 ETS No 158.

of EU law it would render the law effectively useless if the person could not enforce the right. Thus, the issue of state liability for damage caused to an individual for a breach of EU law for which the state is responsible becomes a consideration.

The concept of state liability was established not by any particular treaty article but by the court in *Francovich*, where it stated that "a principle of state liability for damage to individuals caused by a breach of community law for which it is responsible is inherent in the scheme of the Treaty."[35] Here the court is saying that state liability does not need to be explicitly addressed in the treaty itself, rather that it is inherently implied therein.

Subsequently, it confirmed that in order for the state to be liable, three essential ingredients must be present. First, the law that has been breached must have conferred a right on an individual; second, the breach must be severe enough to merit the award of damages. As such the state must have "manifestly and gravely" disregarded the limits of its discretion. Third, there must be a causal link between the state's default and the damage sustained by the claimant.[36]

Thus, the state's obligation under EU law does come with sanctions should its failure to implement a law causes sufficient damage. In these circumstances the state may be liable to pay compensation to the individual(s) effected in addition to any fines it may face in the CJEU should the Commission institute proceedings.

---

[35] Case 6/90 *Francovich v. Italian State* [1991] ECR I-5357.
[36] Case 36/93 *Brasserie du Pecheur SA v. Bundesrepublik Deutschland* [1996] ECR I-1029.

CHAPTER 3

The Employment Contract

The Charter of the Fundamental Social Rights of Workers established that the terms and conditions of employment should be set down in law, by collective agreement or within the contract of employment.[1] This charter inspired the adoption of Directive 91/553, which places an obligation on the employer to inform employees of the terms and conditions of their employment through their contract of employment. Unlike in the United States, this places an obligation on the employer to provide to every employee a contract of employment setting out in writing the terms, scope, and entitlements of employment. While most employment relationships in America will be governed by contract law, there is no federal law requiring that minimum detail be provided in writing to the employee as there is within the EU. This applies to every employee who works for remuneration under a contract of employment or a relationship that is deemed to be one of employment. The essential criterion for the directive to be applicable is that there must be an employment relationship. This is an important inclusion as there is a distinction between an employee and an independent contractor in employment law. Generally, an employee has more rights than an independent contractor. For example, protection against unfair dismissal does not apply to independent contractors, vicarious liability does not apply to contractors, and independent contractors often do not have access to maternity/paternity benefit, sick pay, and so forth. Consequently, it is often beneficial to the employer to have a person deemed an independent contractor rather than an employee. Therefore, the courts have devised a number of tests to determine whether a person is in fact an independent contractor or an employee, regardless of the label attached to the relationship.

---

[1] [1989] OJ C248/1.

The Control Test was one of the earliest tests established by the court to determine the employment relationship. It looked at the amount of control the employer had over the worker. It asked the questions: Can the worker choose his or her own hours or place of work? Does the worker have the option or ability to increase wages? Can the worker hire or fire staff? Does the worker provide his or her own tools? Does the worker have any discretion over how the work is performed? In addressing these questions the court would determine the level of control that the employer had—the higher the level of control the more likely the worker was to be an employee. The Integration Test was developed due to the recognition that the Control Test was not sufficient in all circumstances, particularly where the workers were specialists in a field of knowledge outside of that of their employer. Thus, the integration test looks at whether the work being done is an integral part of the business. The Economic Reality Test looks at things from a different perspective. Instead of looking for evidence of an employment relationship, it looks for evidence of self-employment. Does the worker take any financial risks? Does he or she send invoices or provide equipment? Does the worker provide cover when on leave? The court then moved on to devise the Mutuality of Obligation Test. This test effectively looks at whether the employer is obliged to provide work and whether the worker is obliged to accept it. If there is such an obligation, there is a contract of employment. In more recent years the court has preferred to use the Multiple Test, which is somewhat of a hybrid of the foregoing tests. The court can look at all of the tests and consider the whole situation before coming to a conclusion. This test has proven to be the fairest and most comprehensive to determine whether the worker is an employee or an independent contractor as the court can take all of the elements into account before coming to a decision.[2]

Once the relationship of employment is established, the directive applies to all types of employment, including part-time work and temporary contracts. Contracts of employment that will last for less than one month are excluded as are certain types of casual employment. In the case

[2] Jones, L. 2015. *Introduction to Business Law,* 3rd ed. 429. London: Oxford University Press.

of casual employment, the employer must justify why the directive does not apply.[3]

Article 2 of the directive sets out employer obligations. Paragraph 1 states that the employer must provide information on "the essential aspects of the contract or employment relationship." The CJEU has interpreted this to mean "all aspects of the contacts or employment relations which are, by virtue of their nature, essential elements."[4] Paragraph 2 comprises a nonexhaustive sample list of the matters referred to in paragraph 1 that an employer must provide. These include:

- Names of parties to the contract. If the employer is trading under a name different from that registered, the official registered name must be included in the information
- The primary place of work
- Specification of the job description to include job title and grade attached to it if applicable
- Date of commencement of the employment contract and its duration, including any probationary period
- Entitlements to paid leave
- Notice periods for termination of the contract of employment by both employee and employer
- Rate of remuneration to include any bonus schemes, incremental increases, and frequency of pay
- Hours of work

The employer must furnish this information in writing within two months of commencement of employment. If collective agreements are relevant to the employee and govern his or her conditions of work, these must be indicated to the employee. Any changes to the employment contract must also be given in writing no later than one month after the changes have come into effect. If these changes have occurred due to legislative changes, collective agreement, or administrative regulation,

---

[3] Watson, P. 2014. *EU Social and Employment Law,* 2nd ed. London: Oxford University Press.
[4] Case 350/99 *Lange* [2001] ECR I-1076.

the employer does not have a duty to provide this information in writing to the employee—it is only where the changes occur as a result of the employer's actions.

In the *Kampelmann* case the CJEU had to determine the importance of the accuracy of information contained within the written terms of employment.[5] In this case the claimants had applied for a promotion based on the grade and category of their current position as contained within their terms of employment. They were refused this promotion as the original terms were inaccurate and their work corresponded with a lower grade than that in their contract. Their case in the German Labour Court was dismissed as they had not provided evidence of the necessary length of service in order to secure promotion. In the CJEU it was found that the description could be factual evidence of the employer's duties but proof of such could not depend solely on this notification. The employers must be able to bring evidence to the contrary.[6] Further, it found that the employee must be able to use this information in national courts as evidence in disputes concerning his or her employment.

In short, if this information is presumed to be correct, the employee can rely upon the terms of employment in a national court where there is a dispute in relation to the employment, but the employer can bring evidence to show that the information is inaccurate.[7]

An employee who is sent abroad to work for a duration in excess of one month must receive the following further information:

- Duration of the term abroad
- Conditions governing repatriation
- Currency in which salary or wages will be paid while abroad
- Any benefits in kind to be received while abroad

As this is a directive and not a regulation it does not automatically become part of the domestic law of the member states. Article 8(1) of the

---

[5] Case 253, 254, 255, 265/96 *Kampelmann* [1997] ECR I-6907.

[6] Sargeant, M., and D. Lewis. 2006. *Employment Law*, 3rd ed, 84. Dorchester: Pearson Education Ltd.

[7] Watson, P. 2014. *EU Social and Employment Law*, 2nd ed, 208. London: Oxford University Press.

directive provides that member states are required to introduce measures to give effect to the rights contained therein. Further, it requires the member state to ensure that employees can pursue a claim through a judicial process and have access to redress if the employer fails to comply with employer obligations.

Three further EU Directives are of relevance for the employment contract. First, the Working Time Directive 2003/88 was introduced to protect workers from exploitation by employers. These types of laws are relatively new and come from the recognition that there is unequal bargaining power between an employer and an employee. Historically, these types of legislation were not popular and were seen as an undue encroachment into to the freedom to contract. For example, the Bakeshop Act 1895 was introduced in New York to ensure that employees in bakeries could work no more than 10 hours per day or 60 hours per week. This legislation was predicated on evidence that working long hours in bakeries was having an adverse effect on the health of these workers and the purpose of the legislation was to ameliorate this. This legislation was challenged in *Lochner vs. New York* where the Supreme Court held that the freedom to contract was paramount and that unequal bargaining power was irrelevant. Justice Peckham stated, "It is a question of which of two powers or rights shall prevail—the power of the state to legislate or the right of the individual to liberty of person and freedom to contract. The mere assertion that the subject relates, though but in a remote degree, to the public health does not necessarily render the enactment valid."[8]

This case shows how the courts saw laws that protected employees as an unjustified restriction on the right to the freedom to contract, which was seen as paramount. Small changes began in the United States in 1937 when the Supreme Court in *West Coast Hotel Co. vs. Parrish* upheld the constitutionality of minimum wage legislation in Washington D.C.[9]

Since this time acceptance of the need to impose regulations to ensure safe and just conditions of work has grown. The Working Time Directive ensures that all employees in the EU have:

---

[8] 198 US 45 (1905).
[9] 300 US 379 (1937).

- A minimum of 11 consecutive hours of rest per day
- A rest break where the working day is in excess of six hours
- A minimum one day off per week
- A maximum working week of 48 hours including overtime
- A right to four weeks' paid annual leave
- No more than eight hours of work in any 24-hour period for night-shift workers

There is a significant difference here from U.S. law, where there is no statutory paid annual leave. Some private employers offer paid leave, on average 10 days per year after one year of service. The U.S. National Labor Relations Act 1935 allows for the establishment of unions and collective bargaining for working conditions, which assist employees in obtaining paid annual leave. There are no requirements for rest periods and there is no maximum limit on the number of working hours. However, the Fair Labor Standards Act 1938 does stipulate that any hours over 40 in a given week must be paid at 50 percent more than the standard hourly rate.

The Fixed-Term Work Directive 1990/70 aims to protect workers on fixed-term contracts from discrimination and abuse arising out of the use of successive fixed-term contracts. This directive requires member states to establish in law one or more of the following measures:

- Objective reasons justifying the renewal of such contracts
- A maximum total duration of successive fixed-term contracts
- A maximum number of renewals

The Part-Time Work Directive 1997/81 was introduced to ensure that part-time workers would not be treated less favorably than their full-time counterparts. Any difference in treatment must be justified on objective grounds.

Thus, it can be seen that stricter rules apply within the employment contract in the EU than in the United States. Of particular note is the requirement that all key terms of employment be given to the employee within two months of commencement of employment. Further protection given to employees in relation to working hours and annual leave is not present within the American Labor Law system.

In addition to the framework set down by the EU, the ECtHR has played a role in ensuring that employees are not exploited. As stated earlier, only the state can be found liable under the ECHR and this is seen as a derivative responsibility in that the state needs to ensure that the area is regulated to protect the weaker party. This was accepted by the ECHR in the case of *Young, James and Webster vs. UK* where it was found that the state could not hide behind the fact that the closed shop agreement had been concluded between private parties.[10] The view of the state was that this was a private agreement for which it could bear no responsibility. However, the court found that the state needed to ensure sufficient protection of workers and as it had not done so it was liable for a breach of Article 11. Effectively, this means that the state must put in place safeguards for individuals entering into contracts that, due to the weaker bargaining power of the employee, may have far-reaching implications on the enjoyment of their human rights. One route to this is equalizing the bargaining power—give unions more power.[11] The position of the ECtHR in relation to union rights is considered further in Chapter 7.

In addition to providing safeguards in terms of the employment contract, Article 4 of the European Convention contains a prohibition of slavery, servitude, and forced and compulsory labor. For several decades after its inception it was thought that this article would have no relevance in contemporary Europe. However, even with the wide definition of "worker" under EU law, many migrant or undocumented workers fell outside the scope of this definition. In 2004 the European Court of Human Rights delivered its first judgment declaring a breach of Article 4. The case of *Siliadin vs. France* involved the living and working conditions of a migrant domestic worker.[12] The applicant who was from Togo had been brought to France to receive an education; instead, she was kept at home as a domestic worker. She was forced to work seven days a week cleaning the house and looking after three children. She slept on the floor

---

[10] 13 Aug 1981, Series A, No 44.

[11] See De Schutter, O. 2014. "Contracts as Power" In *The European Convention on Human Rights and the Employment Relation*, ed. F. Dorssemont, K. Lorcher, and I. Schomann. London: Hart Publishing.

[12] App No 73316/01 (26 July 2005).

and was almost never paid. When she escaped, she found that French law did not criminalize her employer's behavior. The ECtHR found that this was not slavery as the employers here did not exercise "ownership" over the applicant. Instead, the court classed this as servitude, which is still contrary to Article 4. The importance of this decision is that it shows that Article 4 does not only apply where the state keeps an individual in servitude, but also applies to private relationships. Pivotal to the court's decision was the lack of any national law remedy for the applicant, reinforcing the states' obligation to ensure safeguards and remedies in the private employment sphere. Article 4 was again considered in relation to human trafficking in *Rantsev vs. Cyprus and Russia*. Here the court expanded its ruling in *Siliadin* and determined that the obligations on the state were to ensure legislation is in place to protect against abusive conduct; to protect victims or potential victims of trafficking that the authorities were aware of, or ought to be aware of, given the circumstances; to investigate trafficking regardless of whether a formal complaint has been made; and to cooperate with authorities in other states.

As such there is a duty imposed on the state to ensure that private employment relations do not breach human rights and that they conform to the provisions of EU law and human rights law generally. Failing to ensure this, the state may find itself in breach of its obligations.

CHAPTER 4

Equality and Nondiscrimination

At the heart of European employment laws lie the concepts of Equality and Nondiscrimination. Article 13 of the Treaty of Amsterdam prohibits discrimination on the grounds of race, gender, pregnancy, sexual orientation, religion, disability, or age. Two further directives establish the Employment Equality Framework, which requires states to transpose measures into national law in order to ensure protection from discrimination in employment. Article 21 of the Charter of Fundamental Rights contains a general prohibition on discrimination as does Article 14 of the European Convention on Human Rights.

In this chapter we are going to examine some of the key issues in relation to equality and nondiscrimination.

Equal Pay

The right to equal pay derives from articles 141 and 119 of the original EEC Treaty and is now contained within Article 157 of the Treaty on the Functioning of the European Union (TFEU). It provides that men and woman shall get the same rate of pay for the same work. It is supplemented by Directive 2006/54, which covers the implementation of equal pay in member states.

The original inclusion of equal pay in Article 119 did not carry with it the power to enforce equal pay; rather, it was left to member states to implement this in their national law. This process was fraught with delays and in the interim cases were taken to the CJEU, which shaped the future of equal pay in EU law. One of the most important cases is *Defrenne No. 2*.[1] Defrenne brought a series of three cases against her

---

[1] Case 43/75 *Defrenne vs. Sabena (Defrenne No.2)* [1976] ECR 455.

employer and in the second one she claimed that she was paid less than her male counterparts in contravention of her right to equal pay under Article 119. It was agreed that the work of an air hostess and a cabin steward were identical and thus the issue of discrimination in pay was not disputed. The question before the court was whether the rights in Article 119 introduced directly into national law a provision that could be relied on in the national courts, notwithstanding existing national law provisions. If they did, then at what date did this become effective? The court found that as the principle of equal pay was one of the fundamental principles of the Union, the provisions of the treaty were directly applicable and "give rise to individual rights which the court must protect."[2] Therefore, the right was to be directly effective from the date of the judgment as the principle of nonretrospectivity would not allow it to go back further.

The Equal Pay Directive (75/117), which was designed to secure equal pay, entered into force several weeks prior to the *Defrenne* judgment. This determination did not make the directive redundant; rather, it has served to compliment the treaties in ensuring implementation of equal pay in cases of indirect discrimination. This directive was repealed in 2009 and replaced with the Recast Directive 2006/54. The purpose of this (according to its explanatory memorandum) was to simplify and modernize union law. Under the Recast Directive, many directives relating to equality and nondiscrimination have been brought together and consolidated.

The law provides for equal pay for equal work for male and female workers; however, it does not define what a worker is. The issue came before the CJEU in *Allonby* where the court determined that the term was to be construed widely and to include independent contractors.[3] The employment relationship will be determined on the facts of the case and is not dependent on classification under national law. For example, a person may be classed as self-employed under national law rules but this would not preclude them from being classified as a worker for the purposes of EU law.

---

[2] Case 43/75 *Defrenne vs. Sabena (Defrenne No.2)* [1976] ECR 455 [24].

[3] Case 256/01 *Allonby* [2004] ECR I-873.

The law applies to both public- and private-sector workers. In *Commission vs. Germany*[4] the court found the provisions were "of general application" and therefore applied to public-sector workers, a position that was affirmed in *Gerster*.[5]

The wording of the law on equal pay suggests that its application is limited to situations where men and women are working for the same employer and carrying out the same work for different rates of pay. In cases where there are different rates of pay across an industry with different employers, there is not one single source for the disparity and therefore no one can be held responsible. This is a principle established in the *Lawrence* case where the applicant Mr. Lawrence and 446 colleagues (most of whom were women) challenged different pay in circumstances where the main employer had contracted out to three independent companies who then employed workers on different rates of pay.[6] As the difference couldn't be attributed to one source (there were three employers), the laws could not apply.

What constitutes pay has been interpreted broadly; it is any payment given for work, whether in the form of cash or benefit. It has been held to include, inter alia, sick leave payments,[7] pay received during maternity leave,[8] family and marriage allowance,[9] compensation for unfair dismissal,[10] travel concessions,[11] Christmas bonus,[12] paid leave,[13] redundancy payments,[14] and severance packages.[15] The source of the pay is immaterial. It can result from the contract of employment, collective agreements, ex gratia payments, statutory provisions, or judicial

---

[4] Case 248/83 *Commission vs. Germany* [1985] ECR I-459.
[5] Case 1/95 *Gerstere* [1997] ECR I-5353.
[6] Case 320/00 *Lawrence* [2002] ECR I-7325.
[7] Case 171/88 *Rinner-Kuhn* [1989] ECR 2743.
[8] Case 342/93 *Gillespie* [1996] ECR I-475.
[9] Case 187/98 *Commission vs. Greece* [1999] ECR I-7713.
[10] Case 167/97 *Seymour-Smith and Perez* [1999] ECR I-623.
[11] Case 12/81 *Garland* [1982] ECR 359.
[12] Case 281/97 *Kruger* [1999] ECR I-5127.
[13] Case 360/90 *Botel* [1992] ECR I-3589.
[14] Case 33/89 *Kowlaska* [1990] ECR I-2591.
[15] Case 249/97 *Gruber* [1999] ECR I-5295.

determinations. While the treaty provision does not mention collective agreements, the directives expressly do so, and this is an example of where they are used to supplement the primary law. In *Kowalska* the court found a clause in a collective wage agreement that excluded part-time employees (predominantly female) from severance grants as unlawful.[16] In *Nimz* the CJEU found that where there is an issue of discrimination in a collective agreement, the national court must set aside that provision and not wait for the agreement to be removed through the collective bargaining process.[17]

Ex gratia payments are payments made by the employer where they are not legally or contractually obliged to do so—they are voluntary payments. In *Garland* the court considered the travel facilities given to the family of retired male workers but not female workers. The court found that these payments were connected to the workers' employment and therefore subject to the equal treatment principle.

As per Article 157, the requirement of equal pay is "equal pay for male and female workers for equal work or work of equal value." In *Kenny* the court found that if the pay of one group of workers is significantly lower than that of another group, where they are doing work of equal value and where the lower paid group is predominantly female, there will be a *prima facie* case of discrimination.[18] Where this arises it has the effect of reversing the burden of proof—the employee does not have to show that there was discrimination; rather, the employer must show that there was not. The court has had to look closely at job classification schemes. This is where the employer may evaluate different components of a job in order to justify a difference in pay. The scope of equal work is qualitative—the focus is on the nature of the work performed and absolute parity is not necessary. In *Murphy* factory workers argued that they should be paid the same rate as store laborers. It was established that the female workers' work was of a higher value than that of the male store laborers and therefore the directive was engaged.[19] The court found that to judge otherwise

---

[16] Case 33/89 *Kowlaska* [1990] ECR I-2591.

[17] Case 184/89 *Nimz* [1991] ECR I-297.

[18] Case 427/11 *Kenny* [2012] ECR I-2301.

[19] Case 157/86 *Murphy* [1988] ECR I-673.

would mean that employers could circumvent the law by imposing more onerous tasks for less pay.

Decisions should not be based on qualifications alone; rather, considerations should be had to the work carried out. This issue was dealt with in *Angestelltenbetriebsrat der Wiener Gebietskrankenkass* where the court was asked to determine whether two groups carrying out identical tasks but with different levels of qualification were in fact performing the same work. It found that if two groups with professional training in different areas do different tasks then they are not performing the same work; however, where they perform the same tasks they may be performing the same work, but reference will be had to the particular skill and training of each group. From this case it appears that the court will take qualifications into account in making its determination, but it will never be the sole consideration upon which the court makes its decision.

The prohibition on pay discrimination applies to both direct and indirect discrimination. However, the grounds of this discrimination is limited to sex. These are defined in Article 2 of the Recast Directive as follows:

(a) Direct Discrimination: Where one person is treated less favourably on grounds of sex than another is, has or would be treated in a comparable situation
(b) Indirect Discrimination: Where an apparently neutral provision or practice would put persons of one sex at a particular disadvantage compared with persons of the other sex, unless that provision, criterion or practice is objectively justified by a legitimate aim and the means of achieving that aim are appropriate or necessary

Direct discrimination is easier to prove and it has been determined in the following situations:

- Where a woman received less pay than a man who previously carried out the same work
- Where a man and woman receive the same basic pay but the man is paid a higher salary supplement

- Where retired male employees retain a benefit that is not available to retired female employees
- Where retirement pensions under occupational schemes are paid out at different ages
- Where conditions attaching to survivors' pensions differ
- Where denial of pay increases during maternity[20]

Indirect discrimination can be a little more difficult to prove given that the pay rates on their face will be identical. This, as the definition states, is a measure that appears to be fair but in reality is discriminatory. The first cases of indirect discrimination relating to pay that the court dealt with were in relation to part-time workers who overwhelmingly were women. While protection for part-time workers is now covered by the Part-Time Workers Directive (97/81), prior to its introduction it fell to the CJEU to determine the issue. In *Jenkins vs. Kingsgate* the claimant worked part-time and complained that she was being paid a lower hourly rate than her full-time male colleagues.[21] Those on this part-time hourly rate were predominantly women. The court found that a difference in pay between full- and part-time workers does not automatically result in discrimination and can be objectively justified. However, if in reality it is a means of reducing the level of pay of a particular group and that group is predominantly women, there may be indirect discrimination (remember, the pay discrimination must be on the grounds of sex).

In coming to its decision the CJEU relied heavily on an American Supreme Court case: *Griggs vs. Duke Power Co.*[22] Here the court held that the use of employment tests or qualifications as a prerequisite for employment or promotion (on the face of it a neutral criterion) amounted to racial discrimination as it disproportionately disqualified minority applicants. Justice Burger for the first time wrote of the "disparate impact"

---

[20] Watson, P. 2014. EU *Social and Employment Law*, 2nd ed, 324. London: Oxford University Press.
[21] Case 96/80 *Jenkins Jenkins vs. Kingsgate (Clothing Production) Ltd* [1981] ECR 911.
[22] 401 U.S 424 (1971)

doctrine, which is contained in the Civil Rights Act 1964 and has now been applied to EU law.[23]

Where a successful claim of discrimination in relation to pay has been made, the remedy is not provided for by EU law; rather, it is for national law to fashion the remedy. Practically, the remedy will most often be in the form of monetary compensation. Generally, the amount of damages will be quantifiable and will not pose too much of a difficulty for the court.

In addition to the protection given by EU law, the ESC also prohibits discrimination on the grounds of sex in relation to pay. The provision of equality in general terms of men and women was not originally included in the 1961 Charter; the only explicit reference was found in Article 4.3, which provided for equal pay for equal work. Now contained within Article 20 of the Revised Charter, Section C stipulates that equal treatment and opportunities in matters of employment must be implemented in terms of employment and working conditions, including remuneration.

The system in the EU is not at all dissimilar to that in the United States and, as noted previously, has influenced the development of indirect discrimination in the EU. The first piece of legislation governing equal pay in America was the Fair Labor Standards Act 1938, which made it illegal to pay women less than men based solely on their sex, and can also be litigated under the Civil Rights Act 1964. The equal pay provisions have historically been fewer in America than they are in the EU. While the EU prefers to look at the circumstances as a whole, U.S. legislation sets down a list of what it will look at to determine whether there is a claim for equal pay. Where the EU does not require absolute parity it appears that the American system does. In determining whether equal work was being carried out they will examine experience, training, qualification, skill, levels of physical exertion, accountability, and working conditions. Further, defenses are available to the employer under the legislation and it falls to the employer to show that any discrimination in pay was due to a reason other than sex. Prior to the *Corning* case it was a legitimate defense to

---

[23] See Tourkochoriti, I. 2017. "Jenkins v Kingsgate and the Migration of the US Disparate Impact Doctrine in EU Law" In *EU Law Stories*, ed. F. Nicola and B. Davies. London: Cambridge University Press.

show that lower pay for women was in line with the going market rate.[24] The Ledbetter Act 2009 was introduced to overturn a previous decision of the Supreme Court that held that the claim must be made within 180 days of the discriminatory act first occurring and thus declared the case inadmissible.[25] The act determines that each discriminatory paycheck creates a new actionable offense from which the 180-day time limit will run, regardless of when the discriminatory act began.

The fact that a gender-based pay gap remains, coupled with discriminatory treatment, has led to criticism. It has been argued that America talks of equality as a core value while consistently tolerating inequality in certain groups.[26]

The proposed Paycheck Fairness Act would supplement the strict conditions by making it an offense to pay men and women different rates of pay for substantially the same work and it would also limit the defenses an employer can use. It is harsher on employers, providing expressly for punitive damages for sex discrimination.

Social Security

The court in *Defrenne* determined that social security benefits could not be considered as pay and therefore fell outside of the scope of the Equal Pay Directive as they are not financed exclusively by the employer.[27] It should be noted in this context that we are not talking about rights to social security or rights to an adequate level of social security generally; rather, we are referring specifically to social security rights by virtue of employment, such as sick leave and pension entitlements. The Equal Opportunities Directive (76/207) originally proposed to include social security within its remit but this was dropped due to the diversity of member states' social security systems and the general reluctance to

---

[24] *Corning Glass Works v Brennan* 417 US 188.
[25] *Ledbetter* 43 USSC 2000.
[26] McCormick, M. 2012. "Disparate Impact and Equal Protection After Ricci v Destefano" *Wisconsin Journal of Law, Gender and Society* 27, no. 2, pp. 100–33.
[27] Case 80/70 *Defrenne vs. Belgium (Defrenne I)* [1971] ECR I-445

commit to a principle of equal treatment in this area.[28] As a result the Equal Treatment in Social Security Directive (79/7) came into effect in 1978 and gave member states six years to transpose its objectives into national law. However, even after this unusually long implementation period (states are normally given two years) many member states had still not taken affirmative action to ensure equality between men and women in social security. As a result, this led the CJEU to determine that the directive had direct effect and could be relied upon in national courts. For example, the court in *McDermott vs. Cotter* held that the directive was "sufficiently precise and unconditional to allow individuals, in the absence of implementing measures, to rely on it before national courts as from 23 December 1984."[29] Essentially, the court here is saying that once the six-year period elapsed, regardless of whether the state had taken legislative steps to give effect to the rights, they would become directly effective and applicable in national courts.

As stated earlier, this section is not concerned with social welfare generally and the directive applies to the working population of employed or self-employed persons, those whose economic activity has been interrupted by one of the enumerated risks, and those seeking employment. The essential element is that the person is either in the workforce or actively seeking to enter it. The CJEU has been somewhat generous in determining how long a person can be out of work and retain his or her status as a worker for the purpose of the directive. In *Nolte*, the applicant worked a part-time job until March 1987. In June1988 she fell ill and notwithstanding that she had been out of work for 15 months prior to her illness, the court found that she was someone who normally worked for remuneration and was therefore a worker.[30] Those who have never engaged in economic activity fall outside of the scope of the directive, as do those who have had a break from the workforce for a reason not specified in the directive. In *Johnson*, the claimant had given up work to look after her daughter and

---

[28] Watson, P. 2014. *EU Social and Employment Law*, 2nd ed, 356. London: Oxford University Press.

[29] Case 286/85 *McDermott and Cotter vs. Ireland* [1987] ECR 1-453.

[30] Case 317/93 *Nolte* [1995] ECR I-4925.

did not qualify as a worker as this was not one of the risks (outside of parental and maternity leave, which we will look at later) listed in the directive.[31]

Once the activity engaged in is economic, the level of pay is irrelevant. In *Megner and Scheffer* the court rejected arguments that people on low-hour contracts were not members of the working population.[32] The court found that the fact that the working hours did not meet all of the claimant's financial needs does not prevent him from being a worker and therefore derives protection from the directive.

In the context of a person seeking employment, previous lack of engagement with the workforce or reason for leaving a previous employer is irrelevant.

The schemes covered by this directive relate to employment and apply to statutory schemes that provide financial assistance for sickness, invalidity, old age, accidents at work, and occupational disease and unemployment.

The benefit must be derived from a statutory scheme that may or may not be part of the state's overall social security regime. Whether the benefit falls within this definition may turn on the facts of each case. Two cases from the UK are useful to illustrate the point. In *Taylor* the state argued that winter fuel payments made to those who have reached retirement age was there to assist those who could not pay their heating bills.[33] The court rejected this and stated that as the benefit was given to those who had reached statutory retirement, it went to addressing the risks associated with old age and therefore fell within the directive. In contrast, *Smithson* concerned a dispute over housing benefit.[34] The scheme in question allowed for a benefit that was calculated on the basis of the needs of the applicant versus their actual income. Issues such as sickness or invalidity (as covered by the directive) were taken into account. The court here found that the directive could not be applied. The benefit was intended to compensate the applicant for the gap in income and was not

---

[31] Case 410/92 *Johnson vs. Chief Adjudication Officer* [1994] ECR I-5483.
[32] Case 444/93 *Megner and Scheffer* [1995] ECR I-4741.
[33] Case 382/98 *Taylor* [1999] ECR I-995.
[34] Case 243/90 *Smithson* [1992] ECR I-467.

an autonomous scheme designed to ameliorate one of the risks identified by the directive.

The principle of equal treatment enshrined in the directive means that there can be no discrimination, direct or indirect, on the grounds of sex in relation to the scope of schemes, calculation of payments and contributions, and calculations of increases for spouses and dependents. This directive also applies to discrimination for postoperative transsexuals. In *Richards* the claimant underwent a male-to-female gender reassignment. At the age of 60 she applied for a pension and was refused.[35] Men were only eligible for a pension when they reached the age of 65. The court held that this treatment was discriminatory under the directive. This ruling clearly draws on the case of *Goodwin vs. UK* in the European Court of Human Rights.[36] Christine Goodwin, a postoperative male-to-female transsexual, claimed that the failure to recognize her new gender, the failure to allow her to marry a male partner, and the difference in age at which she could claim her pension violated her rights under the European Convention on Human Rights. The court agreed and shortly after this ruling the UK enacted the Gender Recognition Act 2004, which allows for the new gender to be legally recognized.

Equal treatment is mandatory and cannot be denied even if it affects only a small number of potential beneficiaries. In terms of direct discrimination, the rate of benefit payable, the conditions entitling one to the benefit, and contributions must be identical for men and women. In *Drake*, the claimant was a married woman who worked until mid-1984 at which point she gave up work to look after her severely disabled mother.[37] She made an application for an invalid carer allowance, a benefit payable to persons engaged in the care of the disabled. She was refused this allowance as she was living with her husband. This practice was deemed discriminatory as it would be payable to a man in the same circumstances.

Indirect discrimination arises where the conditions may seem identical but in practice it is more onerous for one gender to attain the benefit.

---

[35] Case 423/04 *Richards* [2006] ECR I-3585.

[36] *Goodwin vs. United Kingdom* (1996) 22 EHRR 123.

[37] Case 150-85 *Drake* [1986] ECR I-1995

In *Teuling Worms* the issue of marital discrimination was raised.[38] In order to access benefits for incapacity three things were considered: marital status, income earned by the spouse, and the number of dependents. The court found that this provision would be discriminatory unless it could be objectively justified as the proportion of women with dependent husbands was significantly lower and therefore men would be paid a higher rate under the scheme.

As aforementioned, there are a number of exceptions to the applicability of this directive. First, occupational social security schemes are not covered, nor are family or survivors benefits. Further, Article 7 provides for a number of derogations that primarily concern advantages given to women and not men, such as benefits a married woman may get as a result of her husband's insurance, lower age for pension attainment, and recognition of women who have not been in employment due to being engaged in raising families.

Different treatment may be objectively justified. For example, in *Commission vs. Belgium*,[39] different rates of benefit were calculated according to family circumstances, which left women being paid less than men. The court found that the state's objective was to take into account different needs of claimants and its action was therefore justified.

Occupational social security benefits fall neither within pay nor within social security directives. Until the seminal case of *Barber* in the CJEU it was assumed that these schemes fell outside of the scope of Article 157 TFEU.[40] In *Barber*, the claimant was part of a pension scheme that entitled him to certain benefits.[41] He was made redundant at 52 but could not get full benefit until 55, whereas a woman in his position could get this benefit at 50. The court found that as this pension was intended to replace the statutory scheme, was negotiated as part of an employment contract, and was financed wholly by the employer, this was pay as per the Equal Pay Directive. The court accepted that its ruling

---

[38] Case 30/85 *Teuling Worms* [1987] ECR I-2497

[39] Case 229/89 *Commission vs. Belgium* [1991] ECR I-2205.

[40] Joined Cases 75 and 117/82 *Razzouk and Beydoun vs. Commission* [1984] ECR I-1509.

[41] Case C-262/88 *Barber* [1990] ECR I-1889.

could cause chaos and gave it prospective effect only. To strengthen this position a protocol to the Maastricht Treaty was adopted establishing clearly that no occupational social security scheme would be considered remuneration before the date of the judgment.[42] As the law developed incrementally through the courts, the Equal Treatment in Occupational Social Security Schemes Directive (86/373) was adopted and entered into force in 1993. The *Barber* case fell within the midst of the implementation period for this directive and it was amended in light of the decision. This directive has now also been incorporated into the Recast Directive.

The European Court of Human Rights does little to add to the body of law in relation to social security. Article 14 is not a stand-alone right and must be pleaded in conjunction with an additional right contained in the convention. It has been used to ensure certain procedural safeguards, as in *Koua Poirrez vs. France* where it was found that differential treatment of social benefits between French and foreign nationals was in breach of Article 14 in conjunction with Article 1 Protocol 1.[43] Further, it has been used to ensure that any entitlements are implemented in a nondiscriminatory manner. The landmark case of *Petrovic vs. Austria* dealt with parental leave entitlement for fathers.[44] The court determined that there was no obligation to provide entitlements such as parental leave under Article 8. However, the fact that Austria granted such entitlements, failing to implement such allowances in a nondiscriminatory manner was a breach of Article 8 in conjunction with Article 14. Notwithstanding this, the court at the time held that the state had not exceeded its margin of appreciation as there was no general consensus among member states[45]—a ruling illustrative of the difficulty in imposing positive obligations in circumstances where welfare provisions vary from state to state.[46]

---

[42] Protocol No 33 TFEU.

[43] (2005) 40 EHRR 34.

[44] (2001) 33 EHRR 14.

[45] (2001) 33 EHRR 14 [37].

[46] Kos, M.M. 2014. "The Protection of the Right to Health under the ECHR: Is Imposing Positive Obligations the Way to Go?" *Queen Mary Human Rights Review* 1, pp. 119–35.

Despite the fact that this case was ultimately unsuccessful, it precipitated further cases, such as *Niedzwiecki vs. Germany* where the court found a violation of Article 8 in conjunction with Article 14 due to differential treatment in child benefit for those who did not hold a residence permit.[47]

In the case of *Markin vs. Russia* it was held that the failure of Russia to give servicemen the parental leave that was allowed to servicewomen amounted to a breach of the convention.[48] It was noted that the foregoing case of *Petrovic* was unsuccessful on the grounds of a lack of consensus between member states, which here was overcome as the majority of member states had legislation in place providing parental leave for both parents.[49]

Equal Opportunity

Equal opportunity for men and women (in employment) was initially encompassed in Directive 76/207 and covered equality in areas of access to employment, vocational training, promotion, and working conditions. This directive was amended by Directive 2002/73 and required transposition into national law by October 2005. In the intervening years between the two directives a considerable body of case law was amassed by the CJEU and the purpose of the second directive was to take account of this jurisprudence and establish it in law for all member states. This directive somewhat bridges the gaps in the previous two directives and covers certain issues that are omitted from the Equal Pay Directive and the Equality in Social Security Directive. Again, the directive only applies to discrimination based on sex and as such sexual orientation is outside of its scope of application. This has also been encompassed by the Recast Directive.

The directive itself is a broadly expressed call for equal treatment of men and women in the following areas:

- Conditions of access to employment, self-employment, or occupation to include selection criteria for appointment and promotion

---

[47] App No 58453/00 (ECtHR, 25 October 2005) [33].
[48] App No 30078/06 (ECtHR, 22 March 2012).
[49] App No 30078/06 (ECtHR, 22 March 2012) [99].

- Access to vocational training (all types and levels), including practical training
- Equality in working conditions, including dismissals
- Nonrestriction of membership or involvement in workers' organizations or trade unions.

The directive applies to both public and private sectors. The issue of the military has proved to be a tricky area for the court in this regard. It has held that compulsory service for men in the German army did not attract the provisions of the Equal Treatment Directive;[50] however, once a person was in the army, it did apply.[51]

The access to employment aspect of the directive has been deemed to have direct effect. It has been interpreted widely to include not only matters prior to employment but also those that materially affect a decision to keep or accept employment. Discrimination in matters relating to accessing vocational training is also prohibited under the directive. In *Schnorbus* it was held that preferential treatment given to male applicants who had completed military service discriminated against women as the service was compulsory for men and not women.[52] Equality in employment conditions applies to all aspects of the employment relationship, including dismissals.

Direct discrimination is where the employer treats one worker less favorably on the grounds of sex. The difference in treatment must be on the grounds of sex. Therefore, where a rule applies equally to both men and women there can be no direct discrimination under the directive.[53] The restriction of household allowances to married couples was held not to engage the directive as the reason for discrimination was marital status

---

[50] Case 186/01 *Dory* [2003] ECR I-2479

[51] Case 273/97 *Sindar* [1999] ECR I-7403 and Case 285/98 *Kreil* [2000] ECR I-69.

[52] Case 79/99 *Schnorbus* [2000] ECR I-10997.

[53] For example see Case 52/02 *Rinke* [2003] ECR I-8349 where medical training must include periods of full-time training was not discriminatory as it applied to men and women equally.

and not sex.[54] In contrast to indirect discrimination, direct discrimination cannot be objectively justified under this directive. In the case of *Kleist* the court found that the discriminatory treatment could not be justified by the objective of reducing unemployment in younger persons.[55]

As we have already seen, indirect discrimination arises in circumstances where a provision appears to be neutral but its application results in discriminatory effect. This discrimination can be justified if it is to achieve a legitimate aim and its measures are proportionate to achieving that aim.[56]

There are a number of generally accepted justifications set out in the Recast Directive. First, if the measure is genuine and determining occupational requirement, which means that certain types of work may be restricted to one sex depending on the nature of that work. In *Commission vs. UK* the court found the restriction on men entering the profession of midwifery a legitimate one.[57] It based its decision on social factors at the time, including the sensitive nature of the position. Whereas, in *Johnston vs. Chief Constable of the RUC* the refusal to allow a female member to be trained in firearms was held to be discriminatory.[58] The second exception is that it will allow seemingly discriminatory measures aimed at protecting women, specifically within the realm of pregnancy- and maternity-related issues. We look at this as a separate issue in Chapter 5. The third and final exception relates to positive discrimination. For example, in *Kalanke* the court considered a German law that stated that where there were two equally qualified candidates (one male and one female) the female candidate was to be appointed in circumstances where men significantly outnumbered women.[59] It found that laws that guarantee women priority went beyond the bounds of the exception. The strict approach taken here

---

[54] Joined Cases 122/99 and 125/99 *P and D and Sweden vs. Council* [2001] ECR I-4319

[55] Case 356/09 *Kleist* [2010] ECR 1-8861.

[56] Watson, P. 2014. *EU Social and Employment Law*, 2nd ed, 356. London: Oxford University Press.

[57] Case 165/82 *Commission vs. United Kingdom* [1983] ECR 3559.

[58] Case 222/84 *Johnston vs. Chief Constable for the RUC* [1986] ECR 1651.

[59] Case 450/93 *Kalanke* [1995] ECR I-69.

was somewhat loosened in *Marshall* where it was found that such a rule would be valid where it is guaranteed that objective criteria have been applied and doing so could potentially weigh in favor of the man.[60]

The Charter of Fundamental Rights of the European Union, given Treaty status under the Lisbon Treaty, enhances the equality provision. Article 21 prohibits discrimination on the grounds of sex and Article 23 requires that equality "must be ensured in all areas," implying that a proactive approach is required of member states.[61] Article 23 is not limited to paid employment and includes work, a concept that could be linked to unpaid labor primarily undertaken by women.

The ESC also calls for equality in relation to matters of employment and occupation (Article 20). As stated previously, the original 1961 Charter only contained reference to equal pay between the sexes; the revised Charter of 1996 expands this to include vocational training, terms of employment, promotions, and access to employment. The article applies to all who are workers and this, following from the reasoning of the CJEU, has been held to include those seeking employment, those undergoing vocational training, and all other potential workers. Arguably, this goes further than the provisions contained in EU law. In terms of access to employment it requires that there be equality at all stages of employment, from advertising, interview and selection, conditions of work, and promotions to termination of the employment relationship.[62] The principle of equality between the sexes has been identified to mean an absence of either direct or indirect discrimination. The term has not been defined in the ESC but the committee has determined that it is a difference in treatment in comparable situations that does not pursue a legitimate aim and is not based on

---

[60] Case 409/95 *Marshall* [1997] ECR I-6363.

[61] Kravaritou, Y. 2012. "Equality Between Men and Woman (Article 23)" In *European Labour Law and the EU Charter of Fundamental Rights*, 39, ed. B. Bercusson. Brussels: ETUI.

[62] Kollonay-Lehoczky, C. 2017. "The Right to Equal Opportunities" In *The European Social Charter and the Employment Relationship*, 366, ed. N. Bruun, K. Lorcher, I. Schomann and S. Clauwaert. Oregan: Hart Publishing.

objective and reasonable grounds.[63] Therefore, unlike the EU, the charter allows for justification of both direct and indirect discrimination. The ESC does not have an exception to the application of the provision in relation to the nature of the work being suited more to one sex than the other. Several countries have found themselves in violation under the periodic reporting procedure for excluding women from underground work, underwater work, or other work of a labor-intensive and arduous nature.[64] Any justification in this regard cannot relate to an entire occupation, but to certain occupational activities that can only be entrusted to a member of a particular sex. Thus, the difference with the aforementioned *Commission vs. United Kingdom* case would be that under the charter men would not be entirely restricted from entering the profession of midwifery, but may be restricted from the specific tasks associated with the profession. The only other exceptions under the ESC relate to the protection of women, again in relation to pregnancy- and maternity-related matters and measures designed to remove de facto inequality.

The state has a duty to ensure and promote equal treatment within its jurisdiction. The obligations require the state to ensure that legislative measures are in place, ensure that there is an appeals system or tribunal that can vindicate the right, and take practical measures to implement all aspects of equal treatment.

The Race Directive

Historically, issues pertaining to race were primarily dealt with in international and national systems. Although members of the EU had signed up to United Nations (Convention on the Elimination of all forms of

---

[63] *Syndicat national des Professions du Tourisme vs. France* Complaint No 6/1999, decision on the merits 10 October 2001.

[64] Kollonay-Lehoczky, C. 2017. "The Right to Equal Opportunities" In *The European Social Charter and the Employment Relationship*, 368, ed. N. Bruun, K. Lorcher, I. Schomann and S. Clauwaert. Oregan: Hart Publishing.

Racial Discrimination and the International Covenant on Economic, Social and Cultural Rights) and Council of Europe (the European Convention on Human Rights and the European Social Charter) documents that prohibited racial discrimination, this did not automatically correlate to adequate and uniform protection. This is due to the difference in legal systems employed by states. In the application of international law, generally a state may be either monist or dualist.[65] Under a monist regime, international treaties automatically form part of domestic law.[66] The Dutch Constitution, having been described as the 'only truly monist system in Europe,'[67] provides an excellent example where the state is obliged to promote the development of the international rule of law.[68] National legislation is not applied where it conflicts with international law;[69] however, courts have no power to nullify, or amend, offending national law—such power rests solely with the government.[70] Thus, where there is a conflict between international and domestic law, international law will prevail.[71]

---

[65] Shaw, M.N. 2014. *International Law,* 7th ed, 21. Cambridge: Cambridge University Press.

[66] Alston, P., and R. Goodman. 2013. *International Human Rights: The Successor to International Human Rights in Context,* 1058. London: Oxford University Press.

[67] Martinico, G. 2012. "Is the European Convention Going to be Supreme? A Comparative Constitutional Overview of ECHR and EU Law before National Courts" *European Journal of International Law* 23, pp. 401–24.

[68] Article 90 of the *Grondwet* (Basic Law).

[69] Article 94 "Statutory regulations in force within the Kingdom shall not be applicable if such application is in conflict with provisions of Treaties that are binding on all persons or of resolutions by international institutions."

[70] Polakiewicz, J., and V. Jacob-Foltzer. 1991. "The European Human Rights Convention in Domestic Law" *Human Rights Law Journal* 12, pp. 65–125. See also Cassese, A. 1992. *International Law in a Divided World.* Oxford: Clarendon Press.

[71] Polakiewicz, J., and V. Jacob-Foltzer. 1991. "The European Human Rights Convention in Domestic Law" *Human Rights Law Journal* 12, pp. 65–125.

In contrast, dualism asserts that international law does not automatically form part of domestic law.[72] In order for it to be enforceable in national courts a positive act by the legislator is required.[73]

If the Netherlands is seen as a truly monist state, Ireland could be called "ultra-dualist,"[74] a position clearly intended by the Constitution.[75] While it accepts international law "as its rules of conduct in its relations with other states,"[76] Ireland requires a positive act by the Oireachtas before any part of international law can be effective domestically.[77]

Given that a core concept of EU law is its supremacy to national law, in order to ensure uniform and effective prohibition of racial discrimination it became clear that positive action on the part of the EU would be required. The EU began making moves in this direction as far back as 1980 with the Joint Declarations of the Institutions against Racism and Xenophobia.[78] However, declarations are generally seen as aspirational documents and are not legally binding. A wave of immigration in the 1990s into Europe highlighted certain racist attitudes of member states and increased lobbying to the EU for action. The group Starting Line Up, which comprised of representatives from over 200 NGOs, drafted proposed legislation in 1992. While this was a well-supported initiative, there was no basis on which it could be adopted as the EU must have competence conferred upon it in a treaty on which to

---

[72] Alston, P., and R. Goodman. 2013. *International Human Rights: the Successor to International Human Rights in Context,* 1058. London: Oxford University Press.

[73] Byrnes, A., and C. Renshaw. 2014. "Within the State" In *International Human Rights Law,* 464, eds. D. Meockli, S. Shah and S. Sivakumaran. London: Oxford University Press.

[74] Hogan, G. 2014. "The Constitution and the Convention" In *Ireland and the ECHR: 60 Years and Beyond,* 75, eds. S. Egan, L. Thornton and J. Walsh. Dublin: Bloomsbury.

[75] Article 29.6 "No international agreement shall be part of the domestic law of the State save as may be determined by the Oireachtas."

[76] Article 29.3.

[77] Article 15.2.1 "The sole and exclusive power of making laws in the State is hereby vested in the Oireachtas; no other legislative authority has power to make laws for the State."

[78] [1986] OJ C158/1.

base its legislation. If the EU has no competence in an area, it cannot legislate. The year 1997 was designated the European Year against Racism and with it came an increase in momentum and the establishment of the European Monitoring Centre on Racism and Xenophobia, which was tasked with gathering information and assisting with policy. Efforts culminated with the adoption of Article 13 of the EC Treaty, by virtue of the Treaty of Amsterdam, which singled out specific grounds of discrimination, including race.[79] The Action Programme against Racism was published by the commission in 1998 and proposals for a directive followed in 1999.

Directive 2000/43 on equal treatment of persons regardless of race or ethnicity (the Race Directive) was adopted in June 2000. It was fast-tracked through the process and achieved final adoption within six months. This speed can be attributed to three factors:

- The lengthy preparation period leading up to adoption;
- Growing concerns over increased levels of overt racism in member states; and
- Indicating to prospective members the EU's commitment to tackling racial inequality.[80]

The purpose of the directive is set forth in Article 1: to establish a comprehensive framework to combat racial discrimination and to implement equal treatment in all member states. The directive sets out the minimum requirements that a state must adopt, but it is free to incorporate a more comprehensive system should it wish. These minimum requirements are not interpreted narrowly, but rather on the basis of the values upon which the directive was founded, allowing for a changing interpretation of minimum standards as society and law evolve.

The Race Directive directs that any law, regulation, or provision contrary to equal treatment must be repealed. The directive was to be

---

[79] European Union: Council of the European Union, *Treaty of Amsterdam Amending the Treaty on the European Union, The Treaties Establishing the European Communities and Related Acts*, 10 November 1997.

[80] Watson, P. 2014. *EU Social and Employment Law*, 2nd ed, 402. London: Oxford University Press.

implemented in national law (in this case all such offending laws, regulations, and provisions were to be repealed) by July 2003. Rather than merely
determining that the directive would have direct effect (as is the case with
most directives when the state misses the deadline), the commission insti-
tuted proceedings in the CJEU where states failed to comply.[81] This again
evidenced the seriousness with which the EU institutions addressed the
issue of racism within member states.

In 2007, while all states had implemented the directive to some
degree, the commission sent opinions to four member states requiring
them to fully implement the directive. The problem areas that they identified included:

- National legislation that restricted application to workplace
  relations whereas the directive prohibits racial discrimination
  in other areas such as social protection, education, and access
  to goods and services
- States had implemented a definition of discrimination
  narrower than that set out in the directive
- Inconsistencies in systems designed to assist victims of
  discrimination
- The right of individuals to assistance with their claims for
  racial discrimination

The Race Directive applies to a wider set of circumstances than the
employment sphere and it applies to all public and private sectors. It
requires equal treatment in the following areas additional to those considered in the employment relationship:

- Social security and health care
- Social advantages
- Education
- Access to and supply of goods, including housing

---

[81] Case 327/04 *Commission vs. Finland Judgment* 24 February 2005; Case 329/04
Commission vs. Germany Judgment 28 April 2005; Case 320/04 *Commission vs.
Luxembourg* Judgment 9 December 2004; Case 335/04 *Commission vs. Austria*
Judgment 4 May 2005.

Thus, this marks a departure from the discrimination on the grounds of sex and is a recognition that discrimination can permeate other areas of life outside of those governed by the employment relationship. It applies to all persons regardless of nationality and prohibits both direct and indirect discrimination on the grounds of race or ethnic origin. The meaning of race or ethnic origin is not set out in the directive and it has been argued that it also encompasses discrimination on the grounds of skin color, even though this is not expressly articulated. Harassment has been found to constitute discrimination under the directive, and it is required to be directed toward a specific individual. In *Ferma Feryn* the court found that statements in general that a particular race would not be recruited were a breach of the directive's provisions.

Under the directive, direct discrimination occurs where one person is treated less favorably than another in a comparable situation on the grounds of race or ethnic origin. No concrete definition has been given to this "comparable situation" and this, as in cases of gender discrimination, has been problematic, as seen in the cases discussed earlier. Indirect discrimination occurs where a practice or provision appears to be neutral but in reality has a disproportionate effect on a particular race.

Issues of indirect discrimination were considered in *Belov*, which involved the placement of meters to measure electricity consumption in two areas that were predominantly occupied by the Roma community.[82] While the court found the case to be inadmissible, the Advocate General disagreed and found that the action was indirect discrimination but capable of justification if it prevented fraud and benefited its customer base as a whole.

There are three justifications contained within the directive. First, treatment that is based on nationality and not race or ethnic origin is excluded. Perhaps this exception was due to member states' fears that work permit schemes could be seen as being indirectly discriminatory. Further, member states wanted to retain control of those entering their jurisdiction and as such the Race Directive applies to those lawfully present within the member state regardless of nationality. Determining whether discrimination has occurred due to race or nationality may be

---

[82] Case 394/11 *Belov* Judgment 31 January 2012.

difficult in certain circumstances. So an employer who pays third-country nationals less than other workers (EU workers will not be included in this as they have rights under free movement of workers; we consider this in Chapter 6) may be treating them differently on the basis of nationality, but it could equally be indirect discrimination on the grounds of race.[83] It will be for the employer to prove that the discrimination was on the basis of nationality rather than race. The second exception is that of occupational requirements. This is a recognition that certain occupations may require performance by a particular race or ethnicity. The final exception is that of positive discrimination. Guidance is taken from the gender discrimination cases in relation to this aspect and must go no further than necessary to achieve a legitimate aim.

The Race Directive specifies that judicial or administrative remedies must be available where there has been racial discrimination. The directive extends the right to bring a claim in this regard to organizations that have legitimate interest in doing so. However, these organizations cannot bring a claim in their own right; there must be an identifiable claimant on whose behalf they are acting.

The ESC does not contain a specific article in relation to racial discrimination. Instead, it is included in the charter's general nondiscrimination article, Article E. This establishes that all of the rights set forth in the charter are to be enjoyed without discrimination as to race, color, sex, language, religion, political or other opinion, national extraction or social origin, health, association with a national minority, birth, or other status. However, it goes on to provide that any different treatment must be capable of objective and reasonable justification. Initially, the reference to nondiscrimination was contained only within the preamble to the 1961 Charter. The inclusion of Article E in the Revised Charter of 1996 reflects the prevailing attitudes at the time and the movements within Europe generally to combat discrimination. Discrimination on the grounds of race is prohibited in relation to all of the rights contained within the charter. Ethnic discrimination has been given special consideration primarily as a result of treatment of the Roma community within several European

---

[83] Bell, M. 2002. "Beyond European Labour Law? Reflections on EU Equality Directive" *European Journal of Law* 8, no. 3, pp. 385–99.

states giving rise to a considerable number of collective complaints to the committee.[84]

Nondiscrimination on Grounds of Religion, Disability, Age, and Sexual Orientation

While the foregoing directives dealt with specific types of discrimination in relation to race and sex, Directive 2000/78 was introduced to create a more general framework of equality. As we have seen in the European Social Charter and the Charter of Fundamental Rights, these issues are grouped together with others and not segregated as they are within the EU. This directive encompasses religion, disability, age, and sexual orientation.

Religion or belief goes beyond organized religions to other philosophical beliefs on major issues such as life, death, and morality not amounting to religion.[85]

Age is not defined in the directive and while the preamble speaks of the elderly and older workers, the court has considered discrimination against young workers under its ambit. Discrimination on the grounds of age may be justified if it is objectively pursuing a legitimate aim.

The concept of disability is not defined in the directive and whether illness counts as a disability is something that the court considered in the case of *Chacon Navas*.[86] The claimant here was declared as unfit for work in the short term and was dismissed shortly afterward. She brought proceedings claiming unequal treatment and the CJEU had to determine whether sickness and disability were the same thing for the purpose of the directive. It found that as the legislature had chosen a term different from sickness, the two could not simply be equated and that the provision of reasonable accommodation in the directive was indicative of the fact that

---

[84] Kollonay-Lehoczky, C. 2017. "The Right to Equal Opportunities" In *The European Social Charter and the Employment Relationship*, 500. eds. N. Bruun, K. Lorcher, I. Schomann and S. Clauwaert. Oregan: Hart Publishing.

[85] Ellis, E., and P. Watson. 2012. *EU Anti-Discrimination Law*, 2nd ed, 36. London: Oxford University Press.

[86] Case 13/05 *Chacon Navas* [2006] ECR I-6467.

it applied to situations that would endure over a long period of time. This does nothing to address the situation when sickness becomes disability. In *HK Denmark* the court drew on the UN Convention on the Rights of Persons with Disabilities and determined that where an illness (curable or incurable) carries with it a limiting characteristic that would affect effective participation in the workplace, such illness can amount to disability.

The directive sets down the minimum requirements. States may implement more favorable conditions but they cannot rely on the directive to reduce levels of protection. The directive is applicable to all public and private sectors and the state must ensure legislative measures are in place to protect all workers from discrimination under the directive.

A new creation of this directive was the introduction of the concept of reasonable accommodation. This is limited to disabled persons who have the right to reasonable accommodation in the workplace so as to have effective access to employment and training.[87] This concept was relatively unknown within the EU; only the UK, Ireland, and Sweden, which had existing legislation, recognized this obligation within their national law, and the directive provides virtually no guidance as to what this reasonable accommodation may entail. The general rule is that employers (private and public) must take measures to enable disabled persons to access, participate in, and advance in employment, unless these measures would impose a disproportionate burden on the employer, which has been held to include a reduction in working hours. Essentially, this reasonable accommodation prohibits an employer from denying a disabled person an opportunity in employment that, with appropriate adjustments, they would be able to carry out. This adjustment cannon impose an unreasonable burden on the employer, and what constitutes an unreasonable burden is a matter of fact that is determined on a case-by-case basis.

---

[87] Watson, P. 2014. *EU Social and Employment Law*, 2nd ed, 423. London: Oxford University Press.

CHAPTER 5

Protection for Pregnant Workers

In 1990 the CJEU delivered a landmark judgment in the case of *Dekker vs. Stichting Vormingscentrum voor Jong Volwassenen,* which found that pregnancy discrimination was an unlawful direct discrimination on the grounds of gender.[1] However, on the same day this judgment was delivered, the court in another case limited its impact. In *Hertz vs. Aldi* it found that protection from such discrimination was limited in time to the length of the national maternity leave.[2] In recent decades it has been a foremost objective of the EU to ensure the health and safety at work of pregnant workers and those who have recently given birth and to ensure that women are not discriminated against in the employment sector on the grounds of pregnancy- and maternity-related issues.

This is one area where there is clear disparity between the treatment of men and women, but such is justified on objective grounds. The EU has focused primarily on ensuring that pregnancy and childbirth do not give rise to discrimination, ensuring that mothers are given a minimum period of maternity leave and assuring rights during that leave period. It aims to ensure substantive protection by reducing inequalities and to "prevent or compensate for disadvantages in the professional career of the relevant person."[3] Achieving this substantive equality often involves a difference in treatment with the pregnant woman receiving more favorable treatment than a male counterpart. For example, a woman cannot be disciplined for taking time off work due to a maternity-related sickness or illness whereas

---

[1] Case 177/88 *Dekker* [1990] ECR I-3941. See E. Ellis. 1991. "Discrimination on the Grounds of Pregnancy in EEC Law" *Public Law*, p. 159.

[2] Case 79/88 *Hertz* [1990] ECR I-3979.

[3] *Alvarez vs. Sesa Start Espana* ETT SA C/104/09.

a man may be disciplined for absence due to illness.[4] However, this is not necessarily gender discrimination as women who are not pregnant can also be disciplined for absences due to illness.

The Pregnant Workers Directive (Directive 1992/85) aims to protect the health and safety of pregnant workers or those who have recently given birth or are breastfeeding. It was adopted pursuant to the Health and Safety Framework rather than the Scheme of Employment Equality Law, and as a result there is a compromise between the interests of business and the right to equality.[5] The directive also makes provision for:

- Health and safety risks at work
- Maternity leave of a minimum of 14 weeks. Member states are free to increase this and Denmark has the highest level of maternity leave at 52 weeks paid by the government, although not always at full salary level.
- Prohibition of dismissal during the period of pregnancy or maternity leave as it is recognized that such dismissal could have detrimental effects on the health and well-being of the woman
- The rights linked to the employment contract, including some payment while on maternity leave

As the directive refers to the pregnant "worker," we must again consider what the term means in the context of this directive. In *Danosa vs. LKB* the CJEU stated that the concept of a worker must be defined objectively—essentially, the worker is someone who performs services for and under the direction of another person and for which he or she receives remuneration.[6] Again, classifying the relationship as one of self-employment under national law will not necessarily invalidate the provisions of the directive. In this case the court found that even if the woman concerned did not constitute a worker as per the directive, her removal based

---

[4] Case 394/96 *Brown vs. Rentokil Ltd* [1998] ECR I-4185.
[5] Mancini, G.F., and S. O'Leary. 1999. "The New Frontiers of Sex Equality Law in the European Union" *European Law Review* 24, no. 4, pp. 331–53.
[6] Case 232/09 *Danosa* [2010] ECR I-11405.

on pregnancy would constitute direct discrimination on the grounds of gender (as only women can become pregnant) and therefore fall foul of EU law. This is the case even where the pregnant woman has not formally informed her employers of the pregnancy—as long as they have knowledge of the pregnancy, she is protected under the directive.

Most issues relating to pregnancy and maternity matters are now brought under the Recast Directive 2006/54 and not the Pregnant Workers Directive. The Recast Directive confirms that any unfavorable treatment of a woman on the grounds of pregnancy or maternity constitutes direct discrimination. The bounds of the directive were explained as follows: "A female worker is protected in her employment relationship against any unfavourable treatment on that ground that she is or has been on maternity leave.... A woman who is treated unfavourably because of an absence on maternity leave suffers discrimination on the ground of her pregnancy."[7] The directive seeks to ensure that pregnant women are not obliged to work night shifts and for a period following childbirth. A pregnant or nursing worker has the right to have her working conditions adapted and where this is not possible, the right to additional leave.

Further, the directive permits member states to introduce specific measures aimed at guaranteeing women particular rights during pregnancy and maternity. This is intended to ensure the implementation of equal treatment for men and women in relation to access to employment and working conditions. Therefore, women cannot be subjected to unfavorable treatment during the exercise of their maternity rights. However, there are two exceptions to this rule, both of which relate to pay. The first exception is that pregnant women on sick leave due to a pregnancy-related illness are not entitled to special pay. They are entitled only to the same amount of contractual sick pay as any other employee and not entitled to full pay where other employees would not receive the same.[8] Further, where a pregnant woman is transferred to alternative duties there is no requirement to continue to pay supplements that are dependent on performing specific functions.[9] Second, women are not entitled to

---

[7] Case 284/02 *Land Brandenburg vs. Sass* [2005] IRLR 147.

[8] Case 66/96 *McKenna vs. North Western Health Board* [1998] ECR I-7372

[9] Case 147/08 *Parviainen* [2010] ECR I-6533.

full pay during maternity leave.[10] The maternity leave benefit is paid by the state and the amount paid varies throughout the member states. For example, in the UK (which offers 52 weeks' maternity leave) maternity benefit is paid at 90 percent of weekly salary for the first six weeks with no upper limit, then a maximum of £140 per week for the remainder of the leave. In Ireland (with 26 weeks' maternity leave) maternity benefit is either €235 per week or the maximum payable under illness benefit, whichever is higher. France has maternity leave of 16 weeks and the maternity benefit is calculated on the basis of the average daily not to exceed €3,269. Many companies choose to pay additional maternity benefit, topping up the state payment to ensure that at least most of the salary is received during leave.

Maternity leave is intended, according to the CJEU in *Thibault and Gassmeyer*, to protect the woman's biological condition during pregnancy and after childbirth and to protect the relationship between a mother and her child in the period following birth.[11] While this is restricted to mothers, there is provision in EU law for paternity leave. In addition, the court has found that a woman should not be disadvantaged, irrespective of the cost or inconvenience to the employer. This includes protection from risks to health, protection from discrimination in relation to recruitment and promotion, access to benefits during maternity leave, protection from dismissal on the grounds of pregnancy, and the maintenance of employment rights. In *Greismar* the CJEU affirmed that the situation of a pregnant worker is not comparable to that of a male worker where the advantages are designed to offset any inherent occupational disadvantages she may suffer due to being away from work on maternity leave.[12] Thus, a man cannot complain about discrimination in pay or conditions as his situation is not and cannot be comparable. In *Abdoulaye and Ors* it was argued that paying allowances to women during maternity leave was discriminatory as the birth of a child has implications on the whole family.[13]

---

[10] Case 342/93 *Gillespie vs. Northern Health and Social Services Board* [1996] ECR I-475.

[11] Case 195/08 *Thibault and Gassmeyer* Judgment 11 July 2008.

[12] Case 66/99 *Greismar* [2001] ECR I-9383.

[13] Case 194/08 *Abdoulaye* [1999] ECR I-5723.

The CJEU held that the situation of women on maternity leave was different from that of men and therefore the principle of equal pay did not arise. While it was acknowledged that there was an impact on all members of the family, pregnancy, childbirth, and breastfeeding were physically exclusive to women and therefore there could be no comparison.

It is a breach of the directive to refuse to hire an employee due to her pregnancy. In *Dekker* the company violated EU law for failing to appoint a suitably qualified woman due to the possible adverse effects of her pregnancy; it was irrelevant that the company would suffer adverse consequences from her appointment.[14] As noted earlier, dismissal on the grounds of pregnancy is also prohibited. This protection runs from the beginning of pregnancy to the end of maternity leave. It includes decisions that were made and the preparatory steps taken during maternity leave where the dismissal itself did not occur until after the leave had expired.[15] The cases before the CJEU on dismissal on the ground of pregnancy have been vast, but broadly the court has established a number of key principles:

- The protection applies to contracts of indefinite duration and to fixed-term contracts. In *Melgar* it was determined that the decision not to renew a fixed-term contract on the grounds of pregnancy amounted to direct discrimination.[16]
- A woman is not obliged to tell her employer of her pregnancy. It was confirmed in *Busch* that her reasons for this are irrelevant.[17]
- Protection applies to women undergoing IVF treatment.[18] However, a more restrictive approach was taken by the court in relation to a surrogacy arrangement. In *Z vs. A Government Department* the failure to pay the commissioning mother for time off to care for the baby on the same basis as maternity leave was not discriminatory.[19]

---

[14] Case 177/88 *Dekker* [1990] ECR I-3941.

[15] Case 460/07 *Paquay* [2007] ECR I-8511.

[16] Case 36/99 *Melgar* [2000] ECR I-6049.

[17] Case 320/01 *Busch* Judgment 27 February 2003.

[18] Case 506/06 *Mayr* [2008] IRLR 386.

[19] Case 363/12 *Z* Judgment 12 May 2004.

- A pregnant worker cannot be dismissed for sickness due to pregnancy even where another employee could be dismissed for the same absences due to illness.

The Recast Directive now includes pay as a form of unfavorable treatment; where a woman is paid less when at work because of her pregnancy, this will be discrimination without the need to show that a man doing equal work was paid more.

A woman on maternity leave is entitled to return to the same job and in the same position with terms no less favorable. If she is not allowed to return to her job or if adverse conditions have been added in her absence, this will be discriminatory.

In addition, a woman cannot be deprived of an appraisal and consequently denied the right to apply for a promotion by virtue of being on maternity leave.[20]

Parental leave is a concept that allows parents to take unpaid leave to care for young children. The Parental Leave Directive[21] had a difficult start. It was first proposed in 1983 but was abandoned due to the need for unanimity. Eventually adopted in 1996, it gave the state two years to incorporate provisions. This directive was repealed in 2012 and replaced by the 2010 Directive.[22] The purpose of the new directive is to "facilitate the reconciliation of professional and parental responsibilities for working parents…taking account the increasing diversity of family structures while respecting national law, collective agreements and/or practice."[23] The right to parental leave is for four months for each child and this leave is unpaid. The entitlement is given to parents of a child or adopted child up to eight years of age. The right is an individual one and cannot be transferred from one parent to the other. Employees returning from parental leave have the right to request changes in their working hours or patterns for a certain period. The directive also stipulates that the employee must return to the same or an equivalent position.

---

[20] Case 195/08 *Thibault and Gassmeyer* Judgment 11 July 2008.

[21] 96/42/EC.

[22] 2010/18 EU.

[23] Clause 1.1.

There has not been a great deal of consideration by the CJEU of the Parental Leave Directive. In *Commission vs. Luxembourg* it was found that the period of parental leave cannot be reduced where it is interrupted by another form of leave (maternity leave, for example).[24]

While there are some similarities between the EU and the United States in terms of antidiscrimination provisions in relation to pregnancy; the glaring difference comes with maternity leave. In the United States, the Pregnancy Discrimination Act forbids discrimination on the grounds of pregnancy in relation to any aspect of employment. In terms of inability to perform a task due to pregnancy or childbirth or related issues the employer is to regard the employee as they would any disabled employee. The employer may have to provide light or alternative duties or other reasonable accommodation as per the Americans with Disabilities Act 2008. If a pregnant woman cannot work at all due to pregnancy-related illness, she may be entitled to unpaid leave under the Family and Medical Leave Act. Employers cannot terminate employment on grounds of pregnancy nor can they discriminate in the hiring or promotion process.

Maternity leave in the EU, however, is very different from that in the United States. It is governed by the Family and Medical Leave Act 1993 and provides that new mothers can take 12 weeks of unpaid maternity leave. This is less than the minimum duration of leave mandated by the EU and is entirely unsupported by state payments. Further, this entitlement to unpaid maternity leave is not open to all. In order to qualify the pregnant woman must work in a firm of more than 50 employees, must have been in employment for a period of at least 12 months, and must have worked a minimum of 1,250 hours during those preceding 12 months.

President Trump has stated that he plans to bring in paid maternity and paternity leave; however, at the time of writing no such plans have been implemented. In the event that this does happen, his proposal is limited to three weeks' paid maternity leave, leaving the United States in the last place among OECD countries.

---

[24] Case 519/03 Commission vs. Luxembourg [2005] ECR I-3067.

CHAPTER 6

Free Movement of Workers

The free movement of workers is enshrined in Article 45 of the Treaty on the Functioning of the European Union and is directly effective on member states,[1] both vertically and horizontally.[2] As noted in Chapter 1, the EU at its inception was (and still largely is) primarily concerned with economic policy. Its overarching aim of a free market required the free movement of goods and services from one member state to the next. You need to bear in mind that unlike the USA, which is made up of states within one country, the EU is comprised of separate countries each with their own borders and trade tariffs. The EU harmonized trade and competition law throughout the union to make it easier for member states to trade with each other. As well as the freedom of moving goods and services from one state to the next, in order for the market to flourish movement of workers was also required. Prior to the EU, and in the absence of bilateral agreements between states, a work visa would be required before you could go and work in another state. While seen as another step toward full market integration, unlike movement of goods and services, movement of people brings implications beyond market concerns. The free movement of people confers individual rights on persons in a direct sense, which has contributed to the development of fundamental rights and the concept of EU citizenship. This free movement is governed by the treaties and also by secondary legislation.

First, it is workers who have the right to move freely within the EU. This is established in the primary law of the EU. However, over the years the secondary legislation has weakened the link between economic activity and free movement, with workers now being seen as individual humans

---

[1] Case 41/74 *Van Duyn* [1974] ECR I-1337.
[2] Case 415/93 *Bosman* [1995] ECR I-4921.

with rights rather than as production factors.[3] The definition of a worker has been developed through the case law of the CJEU without reference to national law. In *Hoekstra* the court held that the provision would be deprived of effect if the definition or concept of worker could be fixed by national law.[4] The essential feature of the employment relationship is that for a certain period of time a person performs duties for or under the direction of another person and for which receives remuneration.[5] The work performed must be an economic activity. For example, in *Bettray vs. Staatssecretaris van Justitie* it was found that a person working in a social employment scheme for the rehabilitation of those addicted to drugs was not performing an economic activity as the purpose of such a scheme is purely social.[6]

In *Levin vs. Staatssecrtaris van Justitie* the court found that the definition was not confined to those in employment, but applied also to those actively seeking employment.[7] This case, and ones following it, centered on the claimant already being in the host state, but naturally the question arose as to whether a person moving to a member state for the purpose of seeking employment would be classed as a worker under the treaty. In *R vs. IAT Ex Parte Antonissen* the claimant sought to fight his deportation from the UK to Belgium by stating that he had been searching for employment for six months.[8] The court found that the member state has the right to deport after six months if the person is not in employment, unless that person can provide evidence that he or she is genuinely seeking employment and has a real chance of being successful in that search.

Directive 68/360 on the Abolition of Restrictions on Movement and Residence within the Community for Workers of Member States and their Families more fully establishes the rights and limitations than those contained within the treaty. This legislation was supplanted by Directive

---

[3] Berry, A., M.J. Homewood, and B. Bogusz. 2015. *Complete EU Law: Text Cases and Materials,* 2nd ed, 428. London: Oxford University Press.
[4] Case 75/63 *Hoekstra* [1964] ECR I-177.
[5] Case 66/85 *Lawrie-Blum* [1986] ECR I-2121.
[6] Case 344/87 *Bettray* [1989] ECR I-1621.
[7] Case 53/81 *Levin* [1982] ECR I-1035.
[8] Case C-292/89 *R* [1991] ECR I-745.

2004/38, which amended, replaced, and repealed some older measures. The purpose of the directive is to more fully expand upon the rights contained within the treaty; however, where there is a conflict between the directive and the treaty, the treaty as primary law prevails.

Article 6 of the directive provides that EU citizens and family members are entitled to the right of residence in another member state for a period of three months without the need for formalities or conditions beyond the requirement to hold a valid passport or identity card. This does not confer any rights to social assistance during this time and the state reserves the right to remove the person if he or she becomes an unreasonable burden. Article 7 deals with duration beyond the three-month period. Migrant workers or self-employed retain their residence by virtue of their position as workers. Others (self-funding migrants and students) can remain only where they can show that they have the means to support themselves, which shows a special preference for the economically active. This reflects the concerns of member states in relation to unregulated migration and welfare tourism. In *Elisabeta Dano* the court upheld the refusal of the state to grant social security benefits to a woman who had lived in the host state for five years but had neither worked nor sought employment.[9]

The migrant worker, once settled, cannot be discriminated against. In *Bosman* the case concerned whether UEFA had breached EU law by the implementation of a rule that permitted national football clubs limit the number of foreign players to three.[10] The court found that this rule did not apply to other member states as such would discriminate against players on the basis of nationality. In *Commission vs. Italy* a rule that private security activities could only be carried out by Italian nationals was a breach of Article 45.[11]

The *Bosman* case is an interesting one as it deals with circumstances that are neither directly nor indirectly discriminatory based on nationality and shows that measures that have a substantially negative impact on access to the market will be prohibited. The facts of the case were that Mr. Bosman was a Belgian professional football player employed

---

[9] Case 333/13 *Dano* Judgment 11 November 2014.

[10] Case 415/93 *Bosman* [1995] ECR I-4921.

[11] Case 283/99 *Commission vs. Italy* [2001] ECR I-4363.

by a Belgian first division club. As his contract was due to expire the club offered him a new contract at a drastically reduced salary, which he refused to sign. As no other club showed interest in signing him he contacted a French second division club. A contract was made for a one-year transfer subject to the French club paying a compensation fee. Both contracts were subject to the condition that the transfer certificate be sent in time for the first match, and the compensation fee was also contingent upon this. The Belgian club had doubts about the solvency of the French club and never sent the transfer certificate; as a result Mr. Bosman's contract with that club never came into effect. The Belgian club also suspended him for a year preventing him from playing for an entire season. The question was whether the transfer rules developed by the governing association formed an obstacle to free movement. Even though this rule (like the aforementioned UEFA rule) did not discriminate on the grounds of nationality, it had an impact on limiting the movement of workers and therefore breached EU law. The principle from the case can be summarized as follows: Measures that impede access to employment market for workers are prohibited under Article 45 even if they do not directly or indirectly discriminate on the grounds of nationality. These measures may be justified by reason of public interest if they are legitimate and proportionate.

The one exception to this rule is in relation to public-sector employees. The *Sotgiu* case confirms that this derogation allows member states to restrict access to certain areas of the public sector; however, it does not allow for discrimination once admitted to the sector.[12]

The principle of equal treatment applies not only to access to the job market but also to the conditions of employment. Article 7(1) of the directive confirms that an employee cannot be treated any differently in terms and conditions of employment based on nationality. An example of such direct discrimination can be seen in *Marsmann*.[13] Here Marsmann was a Dutch national residing in the Netherlands but working in Germany. He suffered an industrial accident that reduced his working capability by 50 percent. German law, which prohibited dismissal on these

---

[12] Case 152/73 *Sotgiu* [1974] ECR I-153.
[13] Case 44/72 *Marsmann* [1972] ECR I-243.

grounds, did not include workers residing in another member state; this was found to be discriminatory as this protection only applied to workers residing in Germany. An example of indirect discrimination can be seen in *Ugliola*, which concerned the period of service used to calculate pay or other advantages in a member state.[14] An Italian national employed in Germany asked for his time spent in the Italian military to be used in calculating his seniority for his position in Germany. German law provided that service in the German military would be taken into account for such calculation but was silent in relation to other armies. There was no direct discrimination as non-nationals could join the German army. The court found this to be indirect discrimination as, although the criterion was theoretically applicable to both nationals and non-nationals, in practice it would only be fulfilled by nationals.

Social and tax advantages must also be shared in a nondiscriminatory manner. These social advantages have been broadly defined by the CJEU and are not confined to those that the state confers on workers. For example, in *Cristini vs. SNCF* the defendant was a French railway company that offered discounted fares for large families.[15] Cristini, an Italian resident in France was refused the card on the basis of nationality. The court found this to be contrary to EU law.

The concept of social advantage encompasses not only benefits granted by virtue of a right, but also those that are discretionary.[16]

The court has found that certain social assistance payments are also social advantages. In *Brian Collins vs. Secretary of State for Work and Pensions* the principle of equal treatment was examined.[17] Here it was found that someone who had worked in the host state would be entitled to equal treatment in the social assistance sphere; however, where they had not yet worked the protection of equal treatment would only apply in relation to access to employment. Thus, this somewhat peculiar decision appears to allow for social welfare benefits to be paid as long as the person is genuinely seeking employment. It is difficult to reconcile this case with

---

[14] Case 15/69 *Ugliola* [1969] ECR I-363.
[15] Case 32/75 *Cristini* [1975] ECR I-1085.
[16] Case 65/81 *Reina* [1982] ECR I-33.
[17] Case 138/02 *Collins* [2004] ECR I-2703.

Article 24(2) of the directive, which explicitly states that the host nation has no obligation to provide social assistance for the first three months of residence, and longer for jobseekers. The case of *Vatsouras* attempted to address these inconsistencies and decided that benefits that are designed to facilitate access to the labor market cannot be classed as social assistance as per the directive.[18]

In addition, taxes and tax advantages must be given equally to nationals and non-nationals of an EU member state. This is generally done where residents and nonresidents are treated differently—that is, paying different types of tax or claiming different types of tax relief. In the normal course of things this would be indirect discrimination; however, in taxation this may not be the case as the two may not be in comparable situations.

There are certain derogations or exceptions from the right to move freely and these are generally on the grounds of public policy, public security, or public health.[19] In *Van Duyn vs. Home Office* the applicant was refused leave to enter the UK to work for the Church of Scientology as the state felt that it was a socially harmful organization.[20] The court upheld the decision of the UK giving it a wide scope to classify activities it determined to be socially harmful. This scope was somewhat narrowed in *R vs. Bouchereau* where the court found that a genuine and sufficiently serious threat to public policy affecting one of the fundamental interests of society would have to be shown for any refusal of entry or deportation to fall within the exception.[21]

Thus, the free movement of workers has evolved into the free movement of people. Citizens of any member state are free to travel to any other member state without restriction for a period of three months. Initially the host state had more control over when it could deport a person back to the home state if that person was not economically active. The evolution of the law shows that this, while still a factor, will not be the sole determinative issue. Benefits that are designed to assist a person

---

[18] Case 22 and 23/08 *Vatsouras* [2009] ECR I-4585.

[19] Chapter VI.

[20] Case 41/74 *Van Duyn* [1974] ECR I-1337.

[21] Case C30/77 *Bouchereau* [1977] ECR I-1999.

into employment are to be made available to all, and a person who has worked toward gaining employment will be entitled to the same level of unemployment benefits. This shows that the EU is moving toward more protection for human rights, seeing people as more than mere economic actors.

CHAPTER 7

Trade Unions and Collective Bargaining

The EU does not acknowledge or provide union rights. These rights are seen as collective rights and the EU protects individual rights, such as the employment rights considered in previous chapters, which are conferred on the person, not a group. As noted already, at its inception the Union was created to further business, as a primarily economic entity and not one that was overly concerned with the rights of the individual. While that has changed over the years, the EU has been relatively silent on union rights, neither promoting nor protecting collective bargaining or the right to strike. The right here is known as the freedom of association and is protected in other international law treaties. For example, Article 22 of the International Covenant on Civil and Political Rights provides that "everyone shall have the right to freedom of association with other, including the right to form and join trade unions for the protection of his interests"; the International Covenant on Economic, Social and Cultural Rights at Article 8(1)(a) protects "the right of everyone...to join the trade union of his choice...for the promotion and protection of his economic and social interests"; and the International Labour Organization Convention requires states to actively encourage and promote the full development of collective bargaining.[1]

Since the adoption of the Charter of Fundamental Rights of the EU, which attained Treaty status under the Lisbon Treaty, there has been a slight boost to union rights. Article 12 simply states that everyone has the right to freedom of association, which has been seen as implying a right to form and join trade unions. Article 12 here is identical to Article 11

---

[1] First noted in Article 19 of the Constitution of the ILO in 1944 and has since been included in 10 key ILO documents.

of the European Convention on Human Rights and as such should be interpreted accordingly as per Article 52 of the charter. Thus, the case law of the ECtHR becomes of pivotal importance in relation to union rights and collective bargaining as the charter and the CJEU remain weak in certain elements of protection. For example, while the Treaty of Lisbon altered the status of the charter, providing in one article that it is legally binding and has the same status as other treaties of the EU, the very next sentence qualifies its scope with the caveat "The provisions of the Charter shall not extend in any way the competences of the Union as defined in the Treaties."[2] Therefore, enforcement of the rights contained within the charter is dependent on pre-existing treaty rights. The court in *Laval* did recognize the right to collective bargaining as forming an integral part of EU law;[3] however, it has been noted that enforcement of these outcomes proves to be difficult as the right to collective bargaining essentially is secondary to the business right to enjoy an undistorted labor market, as was the case in *Alemo-Herron*, which has been deemed a vicious attack on the right to bargain collectively.[4]

Member states of the EU have engaged in various levels of engagement with unions and collective bargaining and during the economic downturn some were actively encouraged by the EU-led Troika to disregard or suspend national pay agreements in order to implement austerity measures. Flowing from pressure of neoliberal policies a report by the European Commission's director general for Economic and Financial Affairs recommended decreased bargaining coverage and an overall reduction in the wage-setting power of trade unions.[5]

---

[2] European Union, *Treaty of Lisbon amending the Treaty on European Union and the Treaty establishing the European Community*, 13 December 2007, 2007/C 306/1; Article 6.1.

[3] Case 341/05 *Laval* [2007] ECR I-11767.

[4] Case 499/04 *Alemo-Herron* [2006] ECR I-2397.

[5] Schulten, T. 2013. "The Troika and Multi-Employment Bargaining: How European Pressure is Destroying national collective bargaining systems" *Global Labour Column* available at http://column.global-labour-university.org/2013/06/the-troika-and-multi-employer-bargaining.html

Given that the EU has reverted to type when it comes to union rights and collective bargaining, which has allowed, even encouraged, member states to reduce, restrict, or repeal certain rights, it is essential that we now look elsewhere to ensure the protection and vindication of these rights. Of highest importance is the ECtHR as it is a court with powers of sanction and enforcement. Before examining the jurisprudence of the ECtHR, a brief consideration of the ESC is warranted as it contains a raft of protections in relation to trade unions. Article 5, the Right to Organise, states:

> With a view to ensuring or promoting the freedom of workers and employers to form local, national or international organisations for the protection of their economic and social interests and to join those organisations, the Parties undertake that national law shall not be such as to impair, nor shall it be applied as to impair, that freedom. The extent to which the guarantees provided for in this article shall apply to the police shall be determined by national laws or regulations. The principle governing the application to the members of the armed forces of these guarantees and the extent to which they apply to persons in this category shall equally be determined by national laws or regulations.

Further, Article 6, the Right to Bargain Collectively, states:

> With a view to ensuring the effective exercise of the right to bargain collectively, the Parties undertake:
>
> a) To promote joint consultation between workers and employers;
> b) To promote, where necessary and appropriate, machinery for voluntary negotiations between employers or employers' organisations and workers' organisations with a view to the regulation of terms and conditions of employment by means of collective agreements;
> c) To promote the establishment and use of appropriate machinery for conciliation and voluntary arbitration for the settlement of labour disputes; and

d) To recognise the right of workers and employers to collective action in cases of conflict of interest, including the right to strike, subject to the obligations that might arise out of collective agreements previously entered into.

A considerable number of cases have been brought before the committee under both of these articles and in its periodic reports the committee has expressed strong disapprobation toward states for failing to live up to their charter obligations. However, as noted in Chapter 2, the committee is not a court and has no power to enforce its decision. It can make recommendations that the state change or adopt certain laws or procedures but has no power to ensure that this happens. Nor can it sanction the state or award compensation.[6] In the limited cases where the committee has requested that the Committee of Ministers make a contribution to the costs of the complainant, such requests have been denied.[7]

Article 11 of the European Convention on Human Rights deals with the freedom of assembly and association. It states:

1. Everyone has the right to freedom of peaceful assembly and freedom of association with others, including the right to form and join trade unions for the protection of his interests.
2. No restrictions shall be placed on the exercise of these rights other than such as are prescribed by law and are necessary in a democratic society in the interests of national security or public safety, for the prevention of disorder or crime, for the protection of health or morals or for the protection of the rights or freedoms of others. This article shall not prevent the lawful restrictions on the exercise of these rights by member of the armed forces of the police or of the administration of the state.

In much of the case law of the court, the relationship between the freedom of association and the right to join a trade union has been discussed.

---

[6] *Confédération Française de l'Encadrement vs. France* Complaint No. 9/2000.

[7] For example, see *European Roma Rights Centre vs. France* Complaint No. 15/2003.

Since the 1970s it has determined that the right to form or join a trade union is a special type of freedom of association. In *Young, James and Webster* it stated, "It therefore follows from the text itself that the right to freedom of association is the overall concept, with the right to join or form trade unions as an element of that concept, rather than a separate and distinct right for the purpose of this Convention."[8]

Questions then arose as to the term "association" and while the court does not give a definition, it is widely accepted that this is a voluntary body convened with a common goal demonstrating a minimum level of organization and stability.[9] Determining whether an organization constitutes an association is important in order for the convention to apply. Organizations governed by public law do not qualify as associations. In addition, it can make a difference whether a trade union is addressed as a trade union or an association. If a trade union is, as suggested earlier, a special type of association, then distinct and special rights may apply to it and not to other, more general organizations. However, in much of the case law the court has preferred to refer to the trade union as a plain association, ensuring equality of treatment among all associations.[10] Historically, the application of the convention horizontally was contested. These days the courts generally accept that the state has a duty to protect the rights and freedoms to include ensuring an effective remedy for breach of rights even in the realm of relationships between individuals or associations, especially in the area of closed shop agreements.[11] Positive obligations imposed on the state by way of ensuring industrial relations in the private sector are covered by Article 11.

This issue of closed shops is closely intertwined with the right to form and join trade unions. The court has extended the principle into

---

[8] *Young, James and Webster vs. UK*, EComHR, Report of 14 December 1979, App Nos 7601/76 and 7806/77.

[9] See Tomuschat, C. 1993. "Freedom of Association" In *The European System for the Protection of Human Rights*, 493, eds. R. St J. MacDonald, F. Matscher, and H. Petzold. Dordrecht, Martinus Nijhoff Publishers.

[10] See *Sigurdur A Sigurjonsson vs. Iceland* App No 16130/90 (30 June 1993)

[11] Van Hiel, I. 2013. "The Right to Form and Join Trade Unions" In *European Convention on Human Rights and the Employment Relationship*, 289, eds. F. Dorssemont, K. Lorcher, and I. Schoman. Oregon, Hart Publishing.

a negative right, the right not to join a particular trade union. Though the text of the article only confers a positive right to associate and none of the other rights recognize a corresponding negative (for example, the right to life does not carry with it the correlating right to die),[12] the court has openly recognized a right not to organize or associate. In *Young, James and Webster* the court was faced with its first closed shop agreement. Here the three workers were dismissed because of their refusal to join a trade union that signed a closed shop agreement with their employer after their employment commenced. The court cautiously accepted that Article 11 provided some measure of negative freedom of association. The case was, at this stage, without precedent that the court could pin its ruling on as no international protection relating to the right NOT to associate existed.[13] As a result, the monitoring bodies of the ILO and ESC concluded that this would primarily be left to the discretion of states provided that agreements were as a result of free negotiations. The ECtHR chose not to follow this and felt that "it does not follow that the negative aspect of a person's freedom of association falls completely outside the ambit of article 11" due to the difficulties raised by closed shop practices. The court attached high value to the consequences of the practice of closed shop agreements, such as the loss of employment and the political objections of workers to being aligned with unions. The court has always adopted the view that the convention is a document to be read as a whole and not in isolation and affirmed this stance in coming to its reasoning in this case. It looked at the rights protected under Article 9 (freedom of thought, conscience, and religion) and Article 10 (freedom of expression) in interpreting Article 11. As such, the rights contained within Articles 9 and 10 could effectively only be protected if Article 11 carried with it the negative freedom of association. Therefore, to be included in an association against one's will results in an unjustified interference with personal autonomy.[14]

---

[12] See *Pretty vs. UK* [2002] ECHR 423.

[13] Van Hiel, I. 2013. "The Right to Form and Join Trade Unions" In *European Convention on Human Rights and the Employment Relationship,* 290, eds. F. Dorssemont, K. Lorcher, and I. Schoman. Oregon, Hart Publishing.

[14] See Tomuschat, C. 1993. "Freedom of Association" In *The European System for the Protection of Human Rights,* eds. R. St J. MacDonald, F. Matscher, and H. Petzold. Dordrecht, Martinus Nijhoff Publishers.

In the wake of this case several more cases against the UK were lodged with the court. The majority of these reached a friendly settlement with only one arriving before the court. In *Gibson vs. UK* the applicant was unsuccessful.[15] Of great importance to the court's decision was that his livelihood was not at stake and there was no closed shop agreement.

In *Sigurjonsson* the court considered the obligation requiring membership of a professional organization to attain a taxicab license.[16] This case did not involve a trade union nor was membership of the organization imposed by way of closed shop agreement. The organization was made up of self-employed cab drivers and was imposed by law. Even though it performed some public functions it was deemed to be primarily a private association and therefore fell within the remit of Article 11. The court here surpassed its more tentative reasoning in *Young, James and Webster* and stated unequivocally that Article 11 "must be viewed as encompassing a negative right of association"; however, it stopped short of determining whether this right was on par with the positive one. The court again relied on the loss of livelihood and the claimant's ideological objections to membership, even though these were not political in nature, to find a breach of Article 11.

It was in *Sorensen and Rasmussen vs. Denmark* where the court stopped distinguishing between pre- and post-entry closed shops.[17] Until this point it had refused to be drawn on whether pre-entry closed shops (the requirement to join an association or trade union at the time of taking up a contract of employment) would fall foul of Article 11. This may have been influenced by the fact that many of the member states still operated these pre-entry closed shops and the ILO also viewed them as lawful. In this case the applicants complained of the requirement to join a particular trade union as a condition of taking up employment. While acknowledging that on occasion group interests would outweigh individual interest, the court warned that a balance must be achieved to avoid the abuse of a dominant party. As such, a worker who has union membership as a precondition to employment must also be protected by Article 11 due to the fact that the worker seeking employment is in a more vulnerable position.

---

[15] App No 14327/88 (20 April 1993).

[16] *Sigurdur A Sigurjonsson vs. Iceland* App No 16130/90 (30 June 1993).

[17] App Nos 52562/99 and 52620/99 (11 January 2006).

When it comes to the internal organization of the union, the court has refined the law primarily by relying on the provisions of the ILO Convention. In *Cheall vs. UK* the applicant, a branch secretary of the trade union ACTS, resigned and applied for membership of another union APEX. Due to the fact that he was accepted without observance to the TUC Disputes Principles and Procedures, the Disputes Committee excluded him from membership. He challenged this exclusion civilly but to no avail. He challenged this under Article 11 alleging that the UK had failed to protect him from these measures. It was held that the right to join a union cannot be interpreted as conferring a general right irrespective of the rules of that union. The ILO allows for unions to draw up their own constitutions and establish rules for the admission and expulsion of members. The court did require that the state protect individuals from abuse by a dominant union where the measures were disproportionate or unreasonable. In this case the court found them to be neither. Here we can see the balancing act that the court is doing in trying to use the convention to ensure state intervention to protect a weaker party while at the same time allowing a private association set its own rules for membership.

In *ASLEF*, UK legislation was again before the court; this time it was legislation that prohibited a trade union from expelling a member on the basis of his or her political affiliation.[18] The court reiterated its position that it was for the union to draw up its own list of rules and acted as a counter to the negative freedom of association: "An employee or worker should be free to join or not join a trade union without being sanctioned or subject to, so should the trade union be equally free to choose its particular members." The court opined that it would run counter to the freedom in Article 11 if the unions had no control over their membership and they must be free to decide, in conformity with union rules, matters relating to admission and expulsion.

It was not until 2002 that antiunion matters came before the court in *Wilson, National Union of Journalists and Ors vs. UK,* which centered on British legislation that undermined unions and collective bargaining by offering more favorable conditions to employees who agreed not to be in a

---

[18] *Associated Society of Locomotive Engineers and Firemen (ASLEF) vs. UK* [2007] ECHR184.

union. The court found that the freedom of employees to instruct a union to act on their behalf was an essential feature to the freedom of association and union membership. As a consequence the state needed to ensure that the union was not restrained in any way from providing that function. By providing financial incentives to surrender union rights the state had failed in its obligation to vindicate the rights under Article 11. Again, in *Danilenkov vs. Russia* the court examined various techniques used in order to convince employees to part with their union rights, including reassignment, dismissal, reduction in salary, and disciplinary sanctions.[19] As a result of these measures membership of the union plummeted and the union sought redress, to no avail. The court found that the Russian state had failed to fulfill its positive obligation to adopt effective judicial protection and that individuals subject to discriminatory treatment are entitled to challenge such and to obtain damages or other appropriate remedy.

Another important aspect of Article 11 is the right to bargain collectively. This right has been recognized under a number of international documents, first appearing in the ILO Convention in 1949. It was the ESC that first explicitly provided that all workers have the right to bargain collectively and most recently it has been recognized in the Charter of Fundamental Rights of the European Union. Under Article 11 of the European Convention, this right is not present in the text; rather, the court has interpreted the right to include collective bargaining. Initially the court's view was that it was for the state to determine how the union should be heard, and while collective bargaining may be one of the ways in which unions can protect their members' interests, this did not constitute an element of Article 11.[20] This line of reasoning was maintained by the court until 2008 when the case of *Demir and Baykara* was determined. Here, a Turkish trade union was included in negotiations and concluded a collective agreement. There was, however, no recognition of the freedom to associate in Turkey and in addition no legal framework to protect it. As such the Turkish courts determined that the agreement was

---

[19] App No 67336/01 (30 July 2009).
[20] *National Union of Belgian Police vs. Belgium* (1975) 1 EHRR 578; *Swedish Engine Drivers Union vs. Sweden* (1975) 1 EHRR 617.

void and the employees had to repay the increased wages paid to them under the agreement. Here the court reversed its earlier decision, having regard to the changing international standards and laws, found Turkey to be in breach of Article 11, and heralded collective bargaining as an inherent part of Article 11.

This may seem like a strange concept that the court can just depart from its earlier ruling and is not bound by its own precedent. This kind of dynamic interpretation used by the ECtHR has its origins in many European (and U.S.) Supreme Courts where the highest court is not bound by its own precedent. Thus, any particular interpretation of a convention right by the court is not fixed. The evolutive, or dynamic, interpretation was introduced by the court in *Tyrer vs. UK*.[21] The idea is that the convention is not stagnant and is to be interpreted in the context of contemporary societal conditions. This approach was approved in *Sigurjonsson vs. Iceland* where the court reiterated that "the Convention is a living instrument which must be interpreted in the light of present day conditions."[22] In *Selmouni vs. France* it explained the operation of this concept as "certain acts which were classified in the past as inhuman and degrading treatment as opposed to torture could be classified differently in future."[23] This interpretation is a recognition that as society evolves so too do the concepts of fundamental rights protection. This dynamic interpretation is essential if the convention is to maintain its effectiveness. Societal structures have changed considerably since its adoption and failing to interpret it in light of evolving standards would lead to stagnation.

Union rights have evolved significantly over time within Europe and while they are still not comprehensively addressed by the EU, the ECHR and the ESC provide adequate redress and legal provision.

---

[21] (1978) 2 EHRR 1. The court had previously found that birching did not breach Article 3 and in overruling its previous decision confirmed that the instrument would be interpreted in light of societal changes within the member states.

[22] (1993) 16 EHRR 462 [35].

[23] (2000) 29 EHRR 403 [101].

Bibliography

Alston, P., and R. Goodman. 2013. *International Human Rights: The Successor to International Human Rights in Context.* London: Oxford University Press.

Bates, E. 2010. *The Evolution of the European Convention on Human Rights: From its Inception to the Creation of a Permanent Court of Human Rights.* London: Oxford University Press.

Berry, A., M.J. Homewood, and B. Bogusz. 2015. *Complete EU Law: Text Cases and Materials.* London: Oxford University Press.

Byrnes, A., and C. Renshaw. 2014. "Within the State" In *International Human Rights Law*, eds. D. Meockli, S. Shah and S. Sivakumaran. London: Oxford University Press.

De Schutter, O. 2014. "Contracts as Power" In *The European Convention on Human Rights and the Employment Relation*, eds. F. Dorssemont, K.Lorcher, and I. Schomann. London: Hart Publishing.

Ellis, E., and P. Watson. 2012. *EU Anti-Discrimination Law.* London: Oxford University Press.

Harris, D., and J. Darcy. 2001. *The European Social Charter.* New York: Transnational Publishers.

Hogan, G. 2014. "The Constitution and the Convention" In *Ireland and the ECHR: 60 Years and Beyond*, eds. S. Egan, L. Thornton, and J. Walsh. Dublin: Bloomsbury.

Jones, L. 2015. *Introduction to Business Law.* London: Oxford University Press.

Kaczorowska, A. 2013. *European Union Law.* New York: Routledge.

Kollonay-Lehoczky, C. 2017. "The Right to Equal Opportunities" In *The European Social Charter and the Employment Relationship*, eds. N. Bruun, K. Lorcher, I. Schomann, and S. Clauwaert. Oregan: Hart Publishing.

Kravaritou, Y. 2012. "Equality Between Men and Woman (Article 23)" In *European Labour Law and the EU Charter of Fundamental Rights*, ed. B. Bercusson. Brussels: ETUI.

Mowbray, A. 2012. *Cases Materials and Commentary on the European Convention of Human Rights.* London: Oxford University Press.

Sargeant, M., and D. Lewis. 2006. *Employment Law.* Dorchester: Pearson Education Ltd.

Shaw, M.N. 2014. *International Law.* Cambridge: Cambridge University Press.

Tomuschat, C. 1993. "Freedom of Association" In *The European System for the Protection of Human Rights*, eds. R. St J. MacDonald, F. Matscher, and H. Petzold. Dordrecht: Martinus Nijhoff Publishers.

Tourkochoriti, I. 2017. "Jenkins v Kingsgate and the Migration of the US Disparate Impact Doctrine in EU Law" In *EU Law Stories,* eds. F. Nicola and B. Davies. London: Cambridge University Press.

Van Hiel, I. 2013. "The Right to Form and Join Trade Unions" In *European Convention on Human Rights and the Employment Relationship,* eds. F. Dorssemont, K. Lorcher, and I. Schoman. Oregon: Hart Publishing.

Watson, P. 2014. *EU Social and Employment Law.* London: Oxford University Press.

Articles

Bell, M. 2002. "Beyond European Labour Law? Reflections on EU Equality Directive" *European Journal of Law* 8, no. 3, pp. 385–99.

Ellis, E. 1991. "Discrimination on the Grounds of Pregnancy in EEC Law" *Public Law,* p. 159.

Kos, M.M. 2014. "The Protection of the Right to Health under the ECHR: Is Imposing Positive Obligations the Way to Go?" *Queen Mary Human Rights Review* 1, pp. 119–35.

Mancini, G.F., and S. O'Leary. 1999. "The New Frontiers of Sex Equality Law in the European Union" *European Law Review* 24, no. 4, pp. 331–53.

Martin, N. 2009. "Forty Years of the European Charter; Celebration or Commiseration" *University College Dublin Law Review* 1.

Martinico, G. 2012. "Is the European Convention Going to be Supreme? A Comparative Constitutional Overview of ECHR and EU Law before National Courts" *European Journal of International Law* 23, pp. 401–24.

McCormick, M. 2012. "Disparate Impact and Equal Protection After Ricci v Destefano" *Wisconsin Journal of Law, Gender and Society* 27, no. 2, pp. 100–33.

Polakiewicz, J., and V. Jacob-Foltzer. 1991. "The European Human Rights Convention in Domestic Law" *Human Rights Law Journal* 12, pp. 65–125.

Zuleeg, M.M. 1971. "Fundamental Rights and the Law of the European Communities" *Common Market Law Review* 8, no. 4, pp. 446–61.

Index

OTHER TITLES IN OUR BUSINESS LAW COLLECTION

John Wood, Econautics Sustainability Institute, Editor

- *Preventing Litigation: An Early Warning System to Get Big Value out of Big Data*
  by Nelson E. Brestoff and William H. Inmon
- *Understanding Consumer Bankruptcy: A Guide for Businesses, Managers, and Creditors*
  by Scott B. Kuperberg
- *The History of Economic Thought: A Concise Treatise for Business, Law, and
  Public Policy, Volume I: From the Ancients Through Keynes* by Robert Ashford and
  Stefan Padfield
- *Buyer Beware: The Hidden Cost of Labor in an International Merger and Acquisition*
  by Elvira Medici and Linda J. Spievack
- *The History of Economic Thought: A Concise Treatise for Business, Law, and
  Public Policy, Volume II: After Keynes, Through the Great Recession and Beyond*
  by Robert Ashford and Stefan Padfield

Business Expert Press has over 30 collection in business subjects such as finance, marketing strategy, sustainability, public relations, economics, accounting, corporate communications, and many others. For more information about all our collections, please visit www.businessexpertpress.com/collections.

Business Expert Press is actively seeking collection editors as well as authors. For more information about becoming an BEP author or collection editor, please visit http://www. businessexpertpress.com/author

Announcing the Business Expert Press Digital Library

Concise e-books business students need for classroom and research

This book can also be purchased in an e-book collection by your library as

- a one-time purchase,
- that is owned forever,
- allows for simultaneous readers,
- has no restrictions on printing, and
- can be downloaded as PDFs from within the library community.

Our digital library collections are a great solution to beat the rising cost of textbooks. E-books can be loaded into their course management systems or onto students' e-book readers.
The **Business Expert Press** digital libraries are very affordable, with no obligation to buy in future years. For more information, please visit **www.businessexpertpress.com/librarians**. To set up a trial in the United States, please email **sales@businessexpertpress.com**.

www.ingramcontent.com/pod-product-compliance
Lightning Source LLC
Chambersburg PA
CBHW071115210326
41519CB00020B/6311